Training Student Library Assistants

Morell D. Boone   Sandra G. Yee   Rita Bullard

American Library Association
Chicago and London 1991

Designed by Gordon Stromberg

Composed in TEX by Digital Graphics, Inc. and output on a Varityper 4300P
   phototypesetter

Printed on 50-pound Glatfelter, a pH-neutral stock, and bound in 10-point C1S
   cover stock by Braun-Brumfield, Inc.

The paper used in this publication meets the minimum requirements of American National Standard for Information Sciences—Permanence of Paper for
Printed Library Materials, ANSI Z39.48–1984 ∞

Library of Congress Cataloging-in-Publication Data

Boone, Morell D.
   Training student library assistants / by Morell D. Boone, Sandra
G. Yee, Rita Bullard.
      p.   cm.
   Includes index.
   ISBN 0-8389-0561-7
   1. Student library assistants—Training of. 2. Libraries,
University and college—Administration. 3. Library personnel
management. I. Yee, Sandra G. II. Bullard, Rita. III. Title.
   Z682.4.S89B66 1991   90-27837
   023'.3–dc20   CIP

Printed in the United States of America.

95 94 93 92   5 4 3 2

Contents

Figures

Preface

Student assistants have become an increasingly vital part of the library organization. As library staff members, we not only have daily contact with the student assistants themselves, but also depend on their skills, knowledge, and abilities for the processing of correct information and the smooth flow of operations.

Few of us will ever exist in an "ideal" situation, with unlimited funding and a staff of student assistants with library-related backgrounds and work experience, enthusiasm, perfect attendance, and no outside concerns or distractions, who will stay in the position a minimum of three years. In actuality, we all have to deal continuously with inadequate budgets (including funding for student assistants), patrons and new workers arriving at the same time, students who have never or seldom been in a library before, and workers no one else will hire. The library exists in a state of competition with late-night parties, classes, social activities, families, sports, clubs; in addition, many student workers will remain at the library only until something "better" comes along.

With these facts in mind, we have researched library history to gain a better perspective of problems encountered when training student library assistants. With an effective training program, management of student workers becomes easier. In chapter 1, we present an overview of past works, reviewing their validity in terms of today's libraries, and combine their concepts with appropriate management principles. Chapter 2 discusses the applicability of learning theory to training principles. In chapter 3, preparation for training is outlined, so that trainers will have a basis from which to work. A generic training model is presented in chapter 4; here we discuss both what should be included, as well as appropriate training tools and methods. Chapter 5 outlines specific library areas and suggests practical training applications for each.

We hope to answer these questions: How do students learn best when learning academic library work? How can we develop and control the critical thinking processes of our student assistants? How do we motivate and challenge our student assistants to develop to their full potential in the library setting? How do we deal with the varying maturity levels, cultural differences, educational levels, and abilities of our student assistants? What must we do to achieve the highest level of preparation as we become increasingly dependent on our student assistants within academic library operations? And, as a final note, what might we have available to use in the future to aid us in these endeavors?

This book is designed to be a training manual, from which trainers may select what is useful for their individual needs. The information can be used by both supervisors and trainers to enhance the efficiency of their valuable student workforce.

Chapter 1   Introduction

The employees most often encountered in a library may very well be student workers. They staff the circulation desk, shelve the books, check in the periodicals, and help process book orders. In short, they are found where the patrons are and where the work gets done. Often, they are asked as many, if not more, questions than the reference librarians, and student workers usually attempt an answer whether they know what they're talking about or not. Student workers in the technical service area often determine the ultimate fate of the materials added to the collections. The task of library managers is to train these students in library procedures so that they know when to answer the questions and where to put items, when to proceed on their own and when to seek assistance. Training is critical.

Considerable published information emphasizes the management of student library workers. Although part of this management process often is concerned with training, the training process may be excluded or not given full treatment. Authors stress that each training program must be geared to specific institutions and that many variables must be taken into consideration. While many variables must indeed be considered when designing programs, certain principles are standard and can be adapted to specific institutions. Some of these principles come from library literature on student workers, some from management or training literature, and some from literature on teaching and learning styles. All of these principles will be combined to propose a generic training model that can be used in a variety of situations.

An overview of this topic should include a look at the literature available. In 1985, the *Journal of Academic Librarianship* published a review article on the employment of student workers in academic libraries. In this article, Emilie C. White draws conclusions about the way in which students have been managed and trained over the years. Many early articles (before 1945) emphasized the need to be highly selective in the hiring process, with an eye to students who might eventually decide to enter the library profession. As reported in 1931 by Cecil McHale, applicants not only were asked about their personal reading, but also took a written examination to determine qualifications.[1] This practice may still be used in some institutions, but it is used less frequently because there are fewer students to pick from and because libraries relying heavily on federally funded work study money usually have less choice in the selection.

White goes on to talk about the history of training for student library workers. She says, "academic libraries maintain independence in the training of student assistants in the absence of commercially published guides or training manuals . . . ."[2] While all possible methods of training have been used somewhere, White found that in recent years training has made increased use of new technology (computers, videotapes, slides). She also reminded the reader that those currently undergoing training as student library workers may eventually use this training in their future careers.[3]

White's article emphasizes the key role student workers play in the operations of an academic library. Economics alone is a key factor. If students were paid $3.50 an hour, and a library used 2,000 hours of student help per week, to replace them the library would need to hire an additional fifty full-time people, who would not only demand higher wages, but also benefits. Libraries simply couldn't afford it. In the early eighties, drastic budget cuts occurred that affected permanent staffing levels in libraries. At the same time, federal financial aid programs (work study) for students allowed libraries to hire larger numbers of students due to either total or partial funding from federal monies. Schelley H. Childress interviewed three librarians who felt they had some expertise in student assistant training to determine the value of extensive expenditures of staff time and energy. All those interviewed agreed, as other literature attests, that without the students fewer services and hours would result. Childress found that three methods of training seem to predominate in the field: group orientation; written training materials; and individual instruction. Several other methods were also found to be used, though not so extensively.[4]

Two major studies on the topic provided survey results that measured the training student assistants were receiving. William Williams' master's thesis, "Factors Relating to the Employment of Student Assistants in Major American College and University Libraries" gathered results from 264 colleges and universities with a student enrollment of 3,000 or more. Again, selection of student assistants was recognized as an important factor in the quality of service students were able to provide. He also found that a student "has less than 50% chance that there is a training manual for his use or that his supervisor has any organized plan of instruction for him."[5] Williams also reminded librarians that these same untrained students are probably answering more patrons' questions than they would care to imagine. The image of the library is definitely at stake.

James Edwin Gaines' dissertation, "The Student Assistant in Academic Libraries: A Study of Personnel Administration Practices and Institutional Constraints," also studied selection and training of student assistants, as well as other personnel techniques. Gaines surveyed a random sample of 300 university and four-year colleges, receiving an 81.7 percent return rate. Gaines found that little formal training was taking place. He concluded, "academic librarians, by making such slight use of these personnel techniques, are not doing all they can to improve student assistant performance."[6] Gaines pointed out the benefits of hiring student workers in addition to economics; he indicated that various other authorities in the field pointed out that students are both able and eager to work odd hours, evenings, and weekends, because of class schedules. They also provide the library administration with the opportunity to hear, from the students' point of view, how well the library is serving its clientele.[7]

Gaines and others raise the issue of selecting academic library student assistants in light of federally funded work study programs. Citing an inability to select only the cream of the student applicants (assuming a large number of applicants), and using some sort of selection device such as a test, recommendations, interview, or grades, professionals seem to have lost interest in using accepted personnel techniques. Gaines found that "there has been no significant literature on the subject since well before the mid-1960's, when the College Work Study Program began pouring money into wages for student assistants . . . ."[8]

Training Student Assistants

Although little significant literature on training student assistants exists, interest is again developing as libraries seek to project an image of quality service to patrons. Librarians fully realize that student workers are the ones who will most influence this image. Automation of library services is also causing the library profession to look at how student assistants are trained. With more automated services available, students are no longer called on to perform mostly unskilled jobs. Many of the tasks once designated as unskilled are now automated and require new skills. Automation may initially cause more patron questions, and students must be trained to answer these questions. Although the tasks may be different, the principles and guidelines used to train workers will be nearly the same.

Students working in a library need to understand that they are a part of a "support service" that exists to provide service to patrons. This means that student assistant training must emphasize the role students play in achieving "customer" satisfaction. Included in the training materials should be several organization charts, all developed to define the important part a student worker plays. Each chart should also provide the background needed to describe how important each job, and therefore each employee, is to the organization. Through training, libraries can prevent students from making mistakes that ultimately effect quality of service.

It is especially important that students can feel important (they are important!), that they know how highly the library administration values good service, that they know how their specific jobs fit into the scheme of high quality service, and that they are rewarded for doing a good job. Management literature such as *The Greatest Management Principle in the World* reminds us that, "the things that get rewarded get done."[9] Rewards must be a part of every manager's routine. However, without proper training, students cannot be expected to perform well enough to deserve rewards.

The literature just reviewed emphasizes such principles as selection, training manuals, economics, personnel techniques and organization charts. However, other principles can and should be a part of any training for student assistants, for instance since student workers are often asked to make judgments and decisions, shouldn't they be instructed in the process of critical and logical thinking? This would benefit both the library and the student, as he or she learns to question decisions and evaluate information critically. Ultimately, students will make better decisions and render better service. Training and supervision of student library workers thus should provide techniques and opportunities to use critical thinking skills.

In the classroom, faculty members are interested in motivating students to want to learn their material. What can librarians do to provide motivation so that the student will want to learn how to provide good service to library patrons? Students must learn procedures, regulations, rules, titles, and many other things, some even more complicated than their course work. And yet, managers rarely provide them with motivational techniques to interest them in such learning. How can managers make use of Instructional design strategies in developing training programs that provide intrinsic motivation to learn? Some library staff members have tried to incorporate new technology into the learning situations in the hope of stimulating learning. This is one technique, but others exist.

As managers, librarians often use the management technique of goal setting to guide employees to greater productivity. Shouldn't this technique be applied in the training of student assistants? Students who have a goal to work toward can see small successes on the way. A student who starts out in one area of the library and knows that, with a certain amount of training and experience, he or she can move to another area, to more responsibility, to better wages, or to more interesting work, may be more receptive to instruction, and more motivated to learn the system. Setting goals early in the training provides motivation and rewards for progressing.

Training in time management and self discipline is also important. Students are learning the work ethic and must be trained in its importance; providing the basis for this ethic is an important training principle. Students must be provided the ground rules within which they can function, and be continually monitored with this in mind. Training does not end with one formal session; it continues throughout the student's work life.

Ultimately, the incorporation of the processes of critical and logical thinking skills, motivational strategies, goals, and worker self-discipline rely upon the job's design. A generally accepted management theory in today's working environment notes the compatibility of worker satisfaction and worker productivity. What must each job description contain to provide the student worker with motivation, the opportunity to use his or her critical thinking skills, the development of a work ethic, and still meet the goals and needs of the work unit?

A Diverse Student Workforce

A diverse student workforce presents both opportunities and challenges for the library supervisor or trainer. Typically, students hired to work in the library come from a wide variety of backgrounds and cultures. In addition, they arrive with different levels of intelligence, understanding, experience, and interest in the job. Ages of the student assistants may vary widely now that more adults are returning to school for retraining or new careers.

Opportunities are provided to enhance the students' understanding of each other while working side by side. Promoting the "team" approach to patron service also helps develop a micro social culture within the library framework. Students become friends with other students who may be from another culture (either within the United States or a foreign country), may be much younger or older, may be from a rural setting rather than urban, or may be an honors student or barely making the grades to avoid probation. However, within the work situation everyone comes together to serve the library patrons.

It is a challenge to break the language barrier in some cases, and to use techniques for training appropriate for diverse student backgrounds, cultures, and levels of intelligence. These wide variations are an important factor. Some students are "placed" in the library for their college work study program; they are provided on-campus jobs as part of their total financial aid package. They are essentially guaranteed a job somewhere, but are restricted in the number of hours they can work, depending upon the amount of their grants. Other students are eager to be hired by anyone on campus so they can earn enough to "pay their own way." The interest and enthusiasm shown by these two diverse groups can vary significantly. Work study students are sometimes, but not always, less interested in the work and more difficult to motivate. Training that addresses the motivation of all students to learn and interact is necessary.

Students coming from widely diverse cultural backgrounds also converge in the workplace. The cultural differences may be based on race or environment. For some students it may be their first experience away from a familiar environment. Trainers must be sensitive to issues that may arise due to these differences. In training it is necessary to include exercises that focus on working together. As part of these exercises, it is important to emphasize that diversity is good, and that, rather than ignoring differences, people need to celebrate them.

An increase in the number of foreign students attending classes in the United States is also impacting on the student assistant workforce in libraries. Foreign students need jobs too, and are allowed by the federal government to hold jobs on campus while they attend school. These students can significantly enhance the workforce. They often live on campus and rarely go home for vacation, and so are available (and often eager) to remain on campus and work when no other students are around.

Training for these students poses some interesting problems, especially regarding the language barrier. While careful screening will eliminate any student whose English is poor, communication problems will develop even with those whose English appears to be fine. Using both the written and spoken word often helps alleviate the communication problem as some will read English perfectly while verbal understanding is less and vice versa. Understanding the foreign students when they speak is still a problem, however. Some will be much better at speaking than others, and again, careful screening will place students appropriately. Those who read English and understand but do not speak clearly may be perfect candidates areas that do not directly deal with the public, such as shelvers, and training must take this into account. The trainer should not present material exclusively in either written or verbal formats. Variation of method and presentation, chances for discussion and repeating information back to the trainer, and role playing or simulation are all critical elements when training foreign student workers.

The diversity of student assistant cultural backgrounds mandates that the trainer be aware that not all nationalities learn alike. Wide variations in learning styles exist due to cultural values and practices. This is true of foreign student workers as well as American minority students. While it is appropriate, and even expected, that students will ask questions of the teacher and actively participate in the learning process, in some cultures students are raised to believe that quiet observation and imitation is the key. Rote learning is an acceptable method of instruction in other cultures, and any type of critical thinking or problem-solving activity may be seen as a threat to the teacher. In some cultures, group work is the accepted standard. Asking students to do their own work, or learn without the benefit of group interaction, is a hardship. [10]

Being aware of these differences suggests that a variety of training methods will be important. For example, some students may be comfortable and quickly able to grasp the task at hand when engaged in one type of learning activity, but be uncomfortable or not pay attention when other techniques are used. A variety of learning activities and experiences for all students helps assure that some learning will take place at a variety of times.

Training methods must also cover the interactions that take place with culturally diverse patrons. The student workforce is a representative sample of the library community being served. In as much, training must emphasize the diversity of patrons including culture, experience, backgrounds, and age. Of particular emphasis and difficulty may be two-way interactions between culturally diverse student assistants and culturally diverse students. Included in the training materials should be references to the fact that the population being served is culturally diverse, and thus may have a variety of viewpoints on the service being rendered. Student assistants must be instructed in listening skills in order to hear and understand what is being communicated.

International students may also come from cultures in which females are not considered capable of answering questions or giving assistance. The question of authority may be another difficulty. Students may be just as as capable of resolving a problem as the supervisor in charge, but librarians may not be able to convince an international student of that. [11] Therefore, alerting student assistants to the possibility that these behaviors may occur can be a useful tool in avoiding difficulties later.

Student library assistant training must clearly emphasize: (1) consistent, polite treatment of patrons (wherever they may encounter them); (2) clear, concise diction (not necessarily loud); (3) attentive listening and response; and (4) the fact that sarcasm and ridicule have no place. These are rules for behavior to be used by all students for all patrons; however, they may be especially important when dealing with diverse groups.

With this historical view of student assistant training and additional principles, it is obvious that there is yet a great deal to be developed for successful training. Combining these ideas will provide a useful starting place for training models applicable to many situations.

References

1. Emilie C. White, "Student Assistants in Academic Libraries: From Reluctance to Reliance," *Journal of Academic Librarianship* 11:93–97 (May 1985).

2. White, p. 96.

3. White, p. 96.

4. Schelley H. Childress, "Training of Student Assistants in College Libraries: Some Insights and Ideas," *Arkansas Libraries* 44: 25–26 (Mar. 1987).

5. William H. Williams, "Factors Relating to the Employment of Student Assistants in Major American College and University Libraries" (Master's thesis, Brigham Young University, 1969), pp. 6–7.

6. James Edwin Gaines, Jr., "The Student Assistant in Academic Libraries: A Study of Personnel Administration Practices and Institutional Constraints" (Ph.D. diss., Florida State University, 1977), p. iv.

7. Gaines, p. 27.

8.   Gaines, p. 55.

9.   Michael LeBoeuf, *The Greatest Management Principle in the World* (New York: G. P. Putnam and Sons, 1985), p. 23.

10.   Sally G. Wayman, "The International Student in the Academic Library," *Journal of Academic Librarianship* 9:338 (1984).

11.   Wayman, p. 338.

Chapter 2   Motivation, Learning Styles, and Critical Thinking

Student library assistant training programs that integrate learning theories and job design will successfully train student workers. Classroom instructors make use of these same theories, and when applied here, the theories will give students the incentive to produce excellent results for library patrons. Interesting, relevant, and meaningful training, combined with well-designed jobs, give students a firm base from which to build their own motivational and thinking skills. Training is a teaching and learning process. From it students will gain knowledge not only about the task at hand, but also about use of the library in general. Not only does the library benefit from the well-trained, motivated, thoughtful worker; the worker benefits from additional knowledge, skill, and a general feeling of high esteem.

Motivation

In most cases, students do not approach a library minimum wage job as a learning experience. Librarians must design the training experience to create the appropriate learning environment that will help motivate student workers to become high level performers. In order to do this, it is necessary to ask, "Why would a student want to learn this job?" The answer to this question, combined with instructional motivation theories, can assist in motivating students to perform effectively. Morell D. Boone, author of "Motivation and the Library Learner," reviewed the history of instructional design as it relates to library learning. He stated: "The motives of an individual can be divided into two categories of behavioral measures. The first is performance; it refers to the actual accomplishment of a required task. The second is effort; it refers to whether the individual engaged in action is trying to accomplish the task."[1] In this context, motivation is defined as that which accounts for the arousal, direction, and continuance of behavior. Motivational design for library training programs should include the four basic categories of motivational conditions described by John M. Keller, in his instructional design model (fig. 1). These categories are: interest; relevance; expectancy; and outcomes, or satisfaction.[2] Each category, contains elements directly transferable to library training.

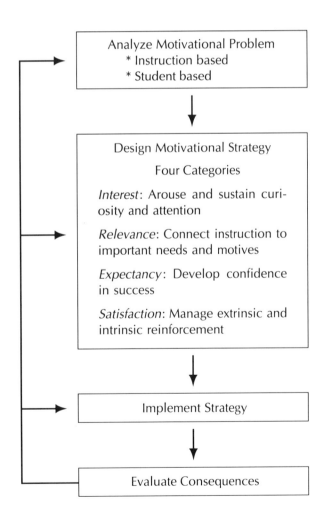

Fig. 1. Designing motivating instruction. From "Motivational Design of Instruction" by John M. Keller in *Instructional-Design Theories and Models: An Overview of Their Current Status* edited by Charles M. Reigeluth. 1983. Hillsdale, N.J.: Lawrence Erlbaum Associates, Publishers. Copyright 1983 by Lawrence Erlbaum Associates, Inc. Reprinted by permission.

Interest

Keller's first category is interest. While many student jobs are something less than interesting, there may be ways to increase interest in the overall process, as well as the specific task. Keller says that epistemic curiosity is of great interest to educators, and thus to librarians. This is information-seeking and problem-solving behavior that occurs as a result of the stimulation of curiosity.[3] In library training, it is important to foster this curiosity and develop skills for problem solving. Librarians can adapt specific techniques to create and maintain curiosity. One important technique is the use of analogies and stories of real, live situations in the training program. Tell the students stories about events that have happened, that involve real people in understandable situations. Draw the students into the situation as much as possible to build an emotional tie. For example, when training students about the importance of all steps in a check-out procedure, the trainer might tell about a book needed by the university president for an important budget meeting. The book was not on the shelf, it was not recorded as being checked out, and there was no time for a long search process. Another copy of the book had to be rush ordered, causing added work for the acquisitions area, the cataloging area, and the budget area. Soon after the book arrived and the president was notified, the same book mysteriously appeared in the book drop. It had been given to a patron with all check out steps complete except one—the step that identified where the book was located. This example can serve two purposes. Not only will it interest the student in a real, live situation, but it can also provide an opportunity to put the students in a problem-solving mode by giving them the chance to arrive at how the problem might have occurred. Students can be guided in a process of question generation, or inquiry, which helps them arrive at a possible solution for the problem. This is also a good time to emphasize the importance of the library's image and the individual's importance to the library's operations.

Relevance

The second motivational category is relevance, or the ability to connect instruction to important needs and motives. These needs could be: power, affiliation, or achievement.[4] In training it is important to provide students with experiences that relate to or might be transferred to the fulfillment of their needs. Many student jobs provide the opportunity for choice, responsibility, and interpersonal influence, all directly related to needs and motives. Job design is critical in this regard. Student jobs can be designed in such a way that choices are provided as to how certain details are handled, or where limited freedom in decision making is allowed. This gives the students the feeling of responsibility and personal influence. It again allows an opportunity for problem-solving, and for decision making skills to be enhanced. Student assistants are put in positions of power in almost every job. They are charged with important responsibilities for helping other students, either when returning items to the shelves, in charging or discharging materials, or in locating required items. This not only affords "power" over their peers, but also provides opportunities for personal influence. Student assistants may not see their jobs in this way unless their vital role is made clear to them during the training process.

The training process will also give potential student assistants a better concept about the library itself: how it works, who to ask for information, where books and other materials are physically located, how to go about checking out materials. This knowledge is not only helpful for the students' own studies, but can also be useful to the assistants' friends and acquaintances. Student assistants can often be seen leading their friends around the library, acting as a personal guide and tutor.

Keller also indicates that students' sense of motivation is higher when a sense of affiliation is developed. [5] Early on in the training program, it is important to build in a sense of the organization, of team work, and the importance of each job to the total operation. Included in written training materials should be organization charts giving the "big picture." Building a "corporate culture" is necessary. Show how important the library is to the university or community, and emphasize the individual student's roles in the organization.

Training programs at McDonald's, Domino's and L. L. Bean are shining examples of building affiliation during training. These corporations realize the benefits of this affiliation to the organization in addition to better-trained employees; and the benefits show up in enhanced customer service. "Trainees are steeped in the Bean culture before they learn policies and procedures," according to the L. L. Bean training supervisor. L. L. Bean reminds its trainees they have a "legend to live up to." [6] While there may be no Leon Leonwood Bean at a particular institution, libraries themselves are often steeped in a tradition that can be built into the training program. Once students truly feel a part of the organization, they can build on their sense of affiliation and trust, and maintain an interest in the training and the job itself.

Expectancy

Expectancy is the third condition for motivated instruction. Expectations of oneself and expectations of others are very important for students when engaged in learning or training. Keller reminds his readers of the "Pygmalion effect," which indicates that clearly defined and demonstrated teacher expectations cause differences in students' achievement levels. [7] This is also known as the "self-fulfilling prophecy." This has serious implications for trainers who work with students of varying levels of intelligence and ability. It is quite clear that a trainer's attitude toward these students can influence the students' expectations of themselves, and cause varying levels of learning to take place. Obviously, library supervisors must give students reason to believe that their success is expected, and that they will learn the appropriate steps necessary to be competent employees.

Hand in hand with expectations of others is expectations of oneself, believing in one's own capabilities for success, also known as a positive self-concept. Foster this in training by providing experience with success early during the training, and by building on this success throughout the work experience. Give each student the opportunity to learn a task, to try the task, to experience success, and to be rewarded in a fairly regular manner throughout the training period.

Keller promotes a strategy for motivational design of instruction that states, "Increase expectancy for success by using instructional design strategies that indicate the requirements for success." [8] This is relatively easy to do in training (or should be) since for each student job there are a set of procedures that clearly spell out what is required. A student shelver can experience immediate success, as soon as he or she grasps the main elements of the classification scheme. The trainer does not need to go through the entire call number and ask a new shelver to place the book on the shelf; instead, it would be appropriate—and would build success—to have the new shelvers sort books by main classification scheme only, be rewarded or praised for correct work, and then move on in increments to the next level. Clearly defined procedures for each task are extremely important for this to become a successful motivational tool in the learning experience.

While believing in the students is extremely important, it will not necessarily be all that is needed for training to be successful. Throughout the training, and beyond, good work must be rewarded. Believe that the students *will* learn their jobs, and reward them for work well done. Management literature is filled with the command "What gets rewarded gets done."

Outcomes

Rewards were mentioned in the previous segment but are equally important for the fourth category of motivational conditions, outcomes or satisfaction with the work. Keller tells his readers that "extrinsic outcomes result from environmental controls and circumstances and intrinsic outcomes result from one's internal emotions and evaluations in response to the performance."[9] Instructional design literature speaks to the use of reinforcement, suggesting that while reinforcement is important, there is reason to be cautious. It has been shown that "extrinsic reinforcement can decrease intrinsic motivation." Student assistants who constantly receive extrinsic reinforcement may come to depend heavily on the expected rewards. If the reinforcement is delivered in a controlling manner rather than informational, intrinsic motivation may decrease. Some suggestions or ways in which this can be avoided in instruction are easily adapted for student library assistant training. Some suggestions made by Keller are: "unexpected, noncontingent rewards; use verbal praise and informative feedback; use motivating feedback; and to improve the quality of performance, provide formative (corrective) feedback when it will be immediately useful, usually just before the next opportunity to practice it."[10]

While all of these suggestions are important, two are especially critical for training. Informative feedback in conjunction with verbal praise is extremely important.[11] It is equally important, however, that it be delivered in an appropriate manner. Condescending manners and tone of voice, even when delivering verbal praise, will not significantly motivate the student. Find something worth praise, be sincere when delivering the praise, and then move into the informative feedback. What has the student done exceptionally well? Why is this the correct procedure? How might it have been done differently but still correctly? In addition to this type of feedback, corrective feedback is also important, but best delivered close to the time it can be meaningful. If a student library assistant at the circulation desk does not properly discharge books, many problems arise. Books may not be "checked-in" with student records cleared, fines may not be recorded, the book may be reshelved without proper clearance. However, catching the student just before he or she leaves for the day, perhaps not to return for several days, is not the best time to provide corrective feedback. Although it may require extra recordkeeping and scheduling effort, it is much more important that this feedback be given to the student just before he or she does this task again. Through the use of both praise and informative feedback, it is possible to impact both the quantity and quality of students' work.

Motivationally speaking, six basic questions need to be answered in planning training programs. Raymond J. Wlodkowski formulated these types of questions as part of his "time continuation model of motivation." They have been adapted to the training of library assistants. The questions are:

1. What can be done to establish a positive attitude?
2. How best can the student be introduced to the training process?
3. What can be done to continuously stimulate the student?
4. How can the emotional climate of the training process be made positive?
5. How does the training increase or affirm student feelings of worth?
6. What can be done to provide the student with continuous positive reinforcement? [12]

Learning Styles

Once students are motivated to learn tasks and procedures, they are ready to participate in a well-designed training program that emphasizes motivational factors. However, to keep them motivated and to provide the best possible learning experience, it is important that the training program incorporate the principles of other learning theories as well. Individual readiness for learning and the various learning styles that students may prefer can be used to enhance the training program and increase the possibility of success. In addition, if students are given the opportunity to recognize their learning styles and to practice learning to learn, they can transfer those skills to academic areas as well as using them in the workplace. Remember: *Student workers are first and foremost students!*

A large body of literature discusses these learning theories and styles. In Gary Mitchell's *The Trainer's Handbook: The AMA Guide to Effective Training* published by the American Management Association, the author recognizes the work of Edward L. Thorndike, whose definitive work on learning serves as a guidepost today. Thorndike delineated three essential laws governing how people learn: (1) the law of readiness—learning occurs only when learners are ready to learn and have the desire, interest, and sufficient skills for comprehension; (2) the law of effect—the importance of success; and (3) the law of exercise—practice and personal involvement. As described earlier, these three laws relate to the conditions that enhance motivation. They are also present and important in the following principles or concepts outlined in the *Trainer's Handbook.*

1. People learn only when they're ready to learn.
2. People learn best what they actually perform.
3. People learn from their mistakes.
4. People learn easiest what is familiar to them.
5. People favor different senses for learning.
6. People learn methodically, and in our culture, systematically.
7. People cannot learn what they cannot understand.
8. People learn through practice.
9. People learn better when they can see their own progress.
10. People learn best when what they are to learn is presented uniquely for them. Each of us is different. [13]

If the training of student library assistants is to be done effectively and efficiently, some attention must be given to each of these principles. Many of these are stated in other (similar) ways in other texts describing learning theory, the hows and whys of student learning. These principles provide a meaningful basis upon which to structure student assistant training.

Students can be prepared for learning the various tasks and procedures of the library through the use of motivational strategies outlined earlier. Students are given information about the library that can be beneficial to them for their studies. Their curiosity can be aroused, and they can garner important information useful to their friends as well as themselves. It is important to include, as will be outlined in chapter 3, the organization of the library (and its various components), how the procedures work, and who to ask when in need of information. All of this serves to provide an answer to the "what's in it for me" question.

In student assistant training, it is easy to incorporate active learning, or practice. It has been suggested in numerous learning theory texts that active learning is usually more efficient than passive learning, perhaps because students are given the opportunity for more feedback. As students are trained in various segments of library procedures, opportunities for practice and appropriate feedback are important. Giving students the opportunity to be successful in early tasks is extremely important. It has been said that students will learn or retain ten percent of what they hear, thirty percent of what they see, fifty percent of what they see and hear. What's even more important, however, is the fact that through the use of active learning techniques, students can increase their percentages of retention to ninety percent of what they see and do. [14]

Closely related to the active learning technique is the value of learning from mistakes. There should be no attempt to ridicule or belittle students who make mistakes. Allowing students to practice procedures and to make mistakes provides an opportunity for them to learn the correct procedure, and probably remember it well. Success is a wonderful reward and can be even more meaningful when it follows an informative correction. For example, if student assistants are learning to shelve materials, they would most likely practice in a confined area before going to the actual shelves. There, they could be allowed some trial and error after initial explanation so that they might be quickly engaged in the activity. Should mistakes occur, which is likely with some complicated shelving arrangements, students have the opportunity to learn from their mistakes and to practice the correct method.

When engaged in learning, students are more likely to understand and remember what is being taught if they can "hook" a concept to some previous experience, or to something that has already been learned. *The Trainers' Handbook* states, "The core skill of training is building bridges that relate new material to the familiar."[15] Student library assistants will very likely have had some type of experience with a library, even if it is not of similar situation or size. The new material and information can build upon the experiences and knowledge already present. Students may have looked for material on shelves; they may have borrowed items and returned them. In the application and interview process, it is possible to ascertain what similar situations may have been present in students' earlier experiences. For specialized areas within the library, it is especially helpful to find out what experience students may have had with audiovisual machines, computers, or photocopy equipment. It is not necessary for them to have had work experience with these things; any experience provides a basis upon which to build.

"All people have an identifiable and preferred learning style."[16] Again, a synthesis of learning style and research indicates that, apparently, when students are taught through resources and strategies complementing their individual preferences, significant increased achievement results.[17] If the training provided for student library assistants takes this information into account, "significantly enhanced achievement" should also result.

Learning Style Modalities

Learning style modalities that may impact instruction include the perceptual, cognitive, emotional, and social. The perceptual and cognitive seem to have the most impact on the training techniques useful for student library assistants and will be investigated in more depth.

**Perceptual
Learning Styles**

The perceptual learning style relates to the way in which learners interact with the environment, and the ways in which they use their senses. There are several elements in the perceptual modality, including: sight (print); hearing (aural); touch (interactive); kinesthesia (motion); visual (observation); and olfactory (smell and taste).[18] All elements except olfactory are important to library assistant training. Students may prefer to see written instructions, procedures, or diagrams as part of the training. These print-oriented students will respond to the procedure manual, especially if it is well documented with charts and samples. For these students, "pictures are worth a thousand words" and the written words are valuable as well. Still other "visual" students learn best by observation. They may prefer (and should be given the opportunity) to observe the procedures being performed by a supervisor or another student. Visual aids such as slides, videotapes and flipcharts also work well for the visual learner, and could be made available as supplements for the training process.

The auditory (aural) learners learn best by listening. They prefer to hear procedures recited to them, either by the supervisor or through a tape. These students will learn extremely well when they hear about the experiences of the supervisor or other student assistants doing a particular procedure or task. It is also important for these learners to be involved in the discourse. While they may absorb the information best by listening to it, they also need to recite the information out loud, or be involved in the discussion in order to reinforce the learning. Therefore, it is not only important that lectures or verbal information be given during the student assistant training, but also that time be allowed for discussion. Encourage the students to talk about what they have just heard or learned and to ask questions about what has been explained.

Interactive learners need to experience that which is being explained. As previously discussed, it is important to provide experiences in which students can touch or physically manipulate the environment. These students will not fully grasp how to shelve a book until they have tried the procedure. In the audiovisual center, these students will not understand the videotape player or film projector until they have worked with them hands-on.

"The kinesthetic individual tends to think as though he can feel the textures and outlines of things encountered in his environment." [19] These students will learn best while moving; in fact, they may actually be processing information while in motion. Kinesthetic learners also prefer to feel the textures of the various objects that require manipulation. It is important for these students to be given the opportunity to "feel" how to charge and discharge books, either by feeling the laser scanners or the actual cards. They will also respond to the active movement of making transparencies or touching the keys on a computer. It is easy to become alarmed with the constant motion exhibited by these students. However, channeled in the right path, movement can be a powerful learning tool.

It is not necessary to survey each student to determine how he or she learns best or that completely individualized training be developed. While it is important that students view the learning situation in an individual way and that they be treated as individuals, training programs should incorporate a wide variety of methods so that the variation in learning styles (perceptual modalities) can be accommodated. Included in student assistant training can be charts, diagrams, written procedures, cassettes or videotapes, transparencies, slides, lectures, discussions, question-and-answer sessions, observation of actual situations, and hands-on practice. With this wide variety of delivery methods students will have the opportunity to absorb material in the modality most comfortable for them.

Anything that can be done to aid the learner in the identification of his or her own learning style will be of benefit in academic areas. Pointing out learning styles to students, as they appear to quickly catch on to a procedure or task presented while using a particular method, can help these students apply that knowledge to their studies and to study more efficiently, to more effectively deal with in-class demands, and to use this additional information.

Cognitive Learning Styles

Cognitive style relates to the learner's typical method of organizing, remembering, and problem-solving. Field independence is a trait of the analytical student as opposed to those who have trouble distinguishing the various parts, and are field dependent. Reflectiveness versus impulsivity is the speed with which a learner reacts to information. [20] In training, it is possible to determine those students who tend to be the more logical, organized thinkers, and who ask more questions. These are the students who can be provided the opportunity to learn the material somewhat more independently. Those who are field dependent would need more direct interaction with the supervisor.

Reflective learners tend to learn in a more systematic way, step by step. This is seen often in our culture. The reflective learner, however, is not necessarily concerned with the speed in which material is grasped, and may be frustrated by trainers who try to move the training along too rapidly. Impulsive learners like speed and are often frustrated by training methods that over-emphasize the step-by-step approach. These students like to be actively engaged in the exchange of ideas and questions. They will function well in situations using role playing and simulations. [21]

Incorporating the cognitive learning styles into student library assistant training requires that the trainer be aware of how information is being given to the students, and whether the students are allowed to make the best use of individual cognitive styles. The training can benefit all types of learners if it incorporates variety. Discussions, question and answer sessions, as well as individual, one-on-one training with the students can provide the needed variety of methods. Individual one-on-one training should also take into account the fact that some learners will react to the information more quickly, and may even disagree on some points. Fostering questioning and promoting logical, analytical thinking can make use of those learners' individual styles and may also lead to better, more efficient procedures.

General Principles of Learning

"Learning takes place only with understanding." [22] Students may be able to memorize procedures but have no concept of the larger picture. In the training of student library assistants, giving them "the big picture" helps them to fit the procedures into a particular context. Giving them the "why" behind the procedures and tasks also helps in recognition and understanding. Training should incorporate some opportunity for the students to demonstrate that they have an understanding of what is really happening. Role playing is an ideal method for checking the students' understanding of some procedures. For example, students working in the audiovisual center may understand the procedures for assisting patrons in making transparencies, but may not understand the reasons for all steps in the process. Using role playing or simulation, the students are expected to be able to ascertain from the patron what needs to be done, and to realize that all component parts are present. This may also require the student assistant to use interview questioning techniques that will demonstrate the ability to understand what is necessary in order to solve a problem.

Some library procedures are so complex that even those students who learn best in analytical situations and who respond quickly to new information may find them beyond comprehension. It is imperative that trainers break these complex procedures into smaller, well-defined segments, so that information overload can be avoided. For example, when explaining the overdue and fine structure, it is important to first establish the length of check-out and overdue information for regularly circulated items. Determining amounts owed for this segment of the collection starts the process that will eventually lead to other types of material with varying loan periods and charges (reserve, audiovisual, etc.). When explaining these complex segments, it helps to relate them to concepts with which students may already be familiar—their public or school library, or even to a nonlibrary example.

While demonstrating complete understanding, student assistants will also be practicing recently learned procedures. Practice with a supervisor, or another already trained student, provides valuable reinforcement and opportunity for feedback. Student library assistants who quickly absorb the information, can demonstrate their understanding of the big picture, and who can successfully perform required functions can be given immediate positive feedback. These students can then be paired with other student assistants who need more instruction and practice. Students training other students can be a very positive, beneficial technique. Peer training can provide a nonthreatening atmosphere from which both students can learn a great deal.

The student assistant training program can make a big impact on students' academic course work if the students are encouraged to use memory and concentration techniques during their training. These techniques can be easily transferred to academic subjects after having been learned and applied during the training. Students will practice learning to learn!

Walter Pauk, author of the popular textbook *How to Study in College*, outlines for students ten principles of learning and remembering. By building in ways of communicating these principles to the student assistants and building in practice and reinforcement of these, not only will training be more efficient, but students will have additional study strategies to take with them outside of the library.

Pauk's ten principles are:

1. *The principle of motivated interest.* Students can be motivated to use the power of interest to work for them.
2. *The principle of goal understanding.* Learn how the specific activity fits into overall library operations. Select general principles and main ideas to remember first, since these involve understanding. Pauk says, "establish a general principle as the magnetic center around which to cluster the supporting details."
3. *The principle of intention to remember.* "The intent to learn is an overall positive attitude that automatically triggers several subsidiary attitudes, such as paying attention, getting a fact right the first time and striving to understand."
4. *The principle of basic background.* The background knowledge is used to bridge new experiences to those already familiar to the learner.
5. *The principle of meaningful organization.* Training must have a logical organization, with some meaningful device for categorizing what is to be learned.
6. *The principle of recitation.* "No principle is more important than *recitation* for transferring material from the short term memory to the long term memory."[23] Simply put, saying aloud the ideas or concepts to be remembered helps move them from the short term memory to the long term memory.
7. *The principle of consolidation.* Consolidation means that an idea or concept is held in mind for four or five seconds, or long enough to allow the concept to jell. Recitation and writing down the concept provide the needed amount of time for consolidation.
8. *The principle of distributed practice.* Distributed practice is that which takes place in short segments of time. Thus, students might spend a short time each day learning and practicing a new skill, but spend additional working time on other tasks.
9. *Use of imagery.* This makes use of the mind's capacity to make mental images. Students can be helped in their mental images through the use of stories and analogies. They can picture themselves in the situations being described.
10. *The principle of association.* New information is tied to old information through the use of mental imagery or sounds. Associations can be made for tasks similar to ones completed outside the library.[24]

In each segment of training there may be an opportunity to highlight or practice one or more of these ten principles. Students can be encouraged often to take notes on what they're learning or to recite back to the supervisor what was recently covered. Short time periods for the actual training are important so as not to overextend the students' mental and emotional capacity and avoid fatigue. Motivated interest in what is being learned is critical. While it is not always possible to incorporate these ideas into the tasks and procedures that must be covered, some attention to learning and remembering will benefit the training program and the students.

Critical Thinking

The ability to think critically and respond in a logical manner is of prime importance in any work situation. Critical thinking skills are now being emphasized throughout the college curriculum in the hope that graduates will possess the ability to analyze situations and information and be able to respond appropriately. While training student library assistants to follow guidelines and procedures, it is also possible to provide training and guidance in critical thinking skills. Giving students the skills with which to make decisions and allowing them the opportunity to make some decisions and to answer some patron questions benefits both the student and the library.

Critical analysis of situations is especially important for any student assistants who will be dealing with the public. Patrons present interesting problems (no identification, not knowing exactly what they want, needing directions). With some training in problem-solving techniques and critical thinking, student assistants can act independently in a responsible manner. They can be encouraged to make decisions that will help develop them into interested and motivated student workers.

As in any subject, giving the students a clear, definitive method of looking at problems is important. It is also important to provide the information necessary to solve the problem, and practice solving problems under supervision so that the process becomes a natural one. Not only does this help the student in his or her work situation, but it will also help in academic areas since the same logical problem-solving methods can be used here as well.

The techniques of critical thinking and problem-solving, and practice in their use, can be built into the training material. But before students can practice they must be given a foundation. When instructing students in the various possible situations that may arise in any of the areas, the following information about critical thinking and problem-solving can be included. John Chaffee, author of *Thinking Critically*, teaches an entire course on critical thinking. Chaffee describes the various activities that are a part of thinking critically as: (1) thinking actively; (2) thinking for ourselves; (3) carefully exploring a situation or issue; (4) being open to new ideas and different viewpoints; (5) supporting our views with reasons and evidence; and (6) being able to discuss our ideas in an organized way. [25] Supervisors and trainers must let the students know that they are expected to perform using their critical thinking capabilities.

In conjunction with the above ideas, student assistants need to be provided techniques to use when solving problems. Library work can present many problems, and training students to be logical, independent thinkers is a good way to prepare them to work alone and thus demonstrate successful mastery of their specific jobs. Building in a problem-solving technique and giving sufficient practice in using it is important. The following model is one example that could easily be built into various aspects of the training program. John Chaffee suggests that students ask themselves the following questions: (1) What is the problem? Define the exact problem by determining the clues, looking at the expected results, and stating the problem clearly and concisely. (2) What are the alternatives? Look at possible answers by determining the boundaries and some possible solutions. Look at the various alternatives and determine the advantages and disadvantages of each. (3) What is the solution? Determine what *can* be done. [26]

Student assistants dealing with problem patrons need to be able to use problem-solving techniques without consciously thinking about them; the skills must be second nature. In training, students need to be given these techniques, be shown how to use them (demonstration), and be given the opportunity to practice them (role playing). Using this problem-solving model not only provides a logical method for dealing with an unpleasant situation, but also helps show the patron that the student assistant is knowledgeable and trying to be of help.

Many questions can be answered and patrons helped if this technique is built into the training. Role playing, the problem-solving method, can be very helpful in giving student assistants the confidence needed to deal with patrons. Librarians know that it is sometimes necessary to play "twenty questions" with patrons to find out exactly what they want. Student assistants can be taught to use the problem-solving method to get at the root of a patron's complaint or problem. They must also be provided with the *information* needed to work toward the solution or to offer alternatives. "What can I do?" can only be answered if students know available options that may ultimately be presented to the patrons as possible solutions.

Giving students a foundation of critical thinking skills and problem-solving techniques requires that supervisors provide clearly stated performance expectations. Students trained to think actively for themselves, to explore situations fully, and to consider all alternatives to problems in a logical manner give the best possible service to the library and its patrons.

Combining what is known about motivation, learning, and critical thinking, and using this knowledge to provide effective library student assistant training, is not an easy task. Building a student workforce with minimal turnover provides the library with a cadre of experienced workers who not only know what they are doing but enjoy doing it. Students who are motivated to learn the library and specific jobs, who become integrated into the social network, and who not only understand but enjoy their work are more likely to remain with the organization.

It is clear that in order to integrate knowledge about instructional techniques, library supervisors must understand motivation, must use a variety of instructional methods, and must carefully plan the complete training program before beginning.

References

1. Morell D. Boone, "Motivation and the Library Learner," in *Bibliographic Instruction and the Learning Process,* ed. Carolyn Kirkendall (Ann Arbor, Mich.: Pierian Press, 1984), p. 38.

2. John M. Keller, "Motivational Design of Instruction," in *Instructional-Design Theories and Models: An Overview of Their Current Status,* ed. Charles M. Riegeluth (Hillsdale, N.J.: Lawrence Erlbaum Assoc., 1983), p. 396.

3. Keller, pp. 401–2.

4. Keller, p. 406.

5. Keller, p. 407.

6. Beverly Gerber, "Training at L. L. Bean," *Training* 25:87 (Oct. 1988).

7. Keller, p. 412.

8. Keller, p. 416.

9. Keller, p. 419.

10. Keller, p. 422.

11. Keller, pp. 423 and 427.

12. R. J. Wlodkowski, *Enhancing Adult Motivation to Learn: A Guide to Improving Instruction and Increasing Learner Achievement* (San Francisco: Jossey-Bass, 1985), p. 258.

13. Gary Mitchell, *The Trainer's Handbook: The AMA Guide to Effective Training* (New York: AMACOM, 1987), pp. 24–25.

14. Mitchell, p. 27.

15. Mitchell, p. 27.

16. Wayne B. James and Michael W. Galbraith, "Perceptual Learning Styles: Implications and Techniques for the Practioner," *Lifelong Learning* 8:20 (Jan. 1985).

17. Rita Dunn and Angela Bruno, "Dealing with Learning Styles," *Education Digest* 51:43 (Apr. 1986).

18. James and Galbraith, p. 20.

19. Rich Walsh and Doug Soat, "How Trainees Learn," *Training* 12:40 (June 1975).

20. Walsh and Soat, p. 41.

21. Walsh and Soat, p. 53.

22. Mitchell, p. 31.

23. Walter Pauk, *How to Study in College*, 3rd ed. (Boston: Houghton Mifflin, 1984), p. 93.

24. Pauk, pp. 90–99.

25. John Chaffee, *Thinking Critically* (Boston: Houghton Mifflin, 1985), p. 52.

26. Chaffee, p. 96.

Chapter 3   Preparation for Training

A formal training program has many components that work together to achieve a well-trained student workforce. Carefully reviewing departmental functions and their interrelationships within the organization provides a foundation upon which training can be built. Defining and hiring an appropriate student workforce lays further groundwork for successful training. These two components combine to give the library the basis upon which to operate a well-structured student training program.

Before the implementation of the training program, each department needs to use serious introspection and follow a needs assessment program to determine both what the department functions are, and what the jobs are. What does a department actually do, and how must it be done? It is also important to determine what jobs will be done by students, as opposed to those done by permanent staff.

Job Descriptions

Job descriptions allow the determination of two important concepts: patterns of workflow, and how various jobs interact with and are dependent upon each other. It is important for student workers to understand job dependencies so that they can feel a part of the organization and can appreciate the importance of each separate task. Giving the student an understanding of the *why* behind the procedure during training helps reinforce motivation to complete tasks, and builds pride in the organization. Also, students need to see the end result of their work in order for them to feel successful, thus giving them further motivation to complete "their" assigned job tasks.

Jobs can be analyzed by many varying methods. In his book *Personnel: The Management of People at Work*, Dale S. Beach gives seven basic ways for gathering job information: (1) observation; (2) questionnaire; (3) interview; (4) checklist; (5) daily diary; (6) conference of experts; and (7) a combination of two or more of these methods. [1]

Observation is perhaps the best method for noting the actual work environment, the equipment and material used, and for learning what the job actually is. However, observation generally needs to be combined with one or more alternative methods in order to gain a full picture of job positions and their interrelationships. A job questionnaire provides staff members the opportunity to express their views of what the job is actually about, and gives a clear view of what misconceptions or miscues the staff may have about their roles. Interviews of several or all staff members may also provide the same type of information as the questionnaire, but take more time. With the use of both the questionnaire and interview methods, it is important to be aware of varying interpretations that can lead to inaccurate and confusing analyses. The checklist method, having the staff member associated with the area check off duties as they are performed during the day, and the daily diary method, having a staff member keep a log of the day's activities as they are performed, are both viable ways of gathering information about job positions. However, they are time consuming for both management and staff, as preparation of checklists and diaries must be completed in advance and the staff must start and stop work many times to record the necessary data. The conference of experts provides a good forum for the viewpoints and job positions but, as with other types of direct input methods, prejudices and personality conflicts must be recognized. [2]

It is clear that a combination of information-gathering techniques is probably the best route to take. Observation plus the direct input of the staff doing the work with the viewpoints of those directly involved with the work area will give a well-rounded overview of the job and its analysis. This will also give regular staff members a chance to participate in the process so that no bad feelings about outcomes are present, and opens the door to any problems that may be present in job interpretation or misalignment.

The information collected is used to prepare job descriptions and position statements. In preparing job descriptions, it is important to keep in mind some fundamental issues: don't create jobs for people unless there is a specific, proven purpose; determine if there are functions that were once important, but no longer belong in the department; and analyze functions with an eye to what isn't being done, to see if there is a valid way to accomplish the task with student workers. Position descriptions are not only used to assign the right person to the job, but are also used to communicate job expectations to staff members. As Charles Labelle states in *Finding, Selecting, Developing, and Retraining Data Processing Professionals through Effective Human Resources Management*, "position descriptions are used to communicate job expectations to employees in terms of job function, responsibilities, organizational relationships, and accountability. This is the first step in showing our employees how they fit into the organization and their value to its operations."[3] Labelle goes on to describe the benefits to the employer in using job descriptions. With a solid job description framework, managers will be less likely to compare one individual to another, rather than comparing the individual to the job. They will also evaluate the entire job position and the necessary employee performance, rather than just a few aspects. Finally, managers will clearly know what the job is, not what they think it should be.

Job Design

The way student jobs are designed affects the workers' motivation and commitment to the job. Ultimately, the work itself must be a major motivator, or must provide for significant positive reinforcement.[4] Therefore, incorporating job design guidelines that enhance motivation will benefit both the worker and the organization.

Student jobs should be designed to be challenging yet not overwhelming. Basic job descriptions can be developed that include a wide variety of tasks. Students may assume varying numbers of tasks depending on their capabilities, and may increase the number and level of tasks as they grow in the job. Caution should be used in determining when additional tasks will either challenge or overwhelm.

Jobs that allow students to complete a full cycle of events provide them with a sense of achievement. The sense of achievement is a basic need that helps promote commitment to the organization. In the organizational chart, students can see how they fit in, and why they are important.

Giving student workers jobs that allow them to make some decisions and feel a sense of responsibility and control over situations provides another motivator. In designing the job, students should not feel threatened by the responsibility, but have a clear frame of reference as to where their responsibility begins and ends. Having some control and decision-making power makes them feel important and useful to the organization. Effective job design will respect the idea of discrete responsibilities. A job consists of functions, and each function is made up of tasks. When tasks are made consistent with one another, they will help students understand the functions or purpose of their job. Guided by this knowledge, students will work with greater self-direction.

Build in to each student job skills that are transferable to their lives outside of work. Students who learn about the library and its various components can use this information to their benefit, and can be of help to their friends.

Jobs should be designed in an overall consistent manner. While each job is unique, all jobs must work together to meet the ultimate goal, getting the job done.

Developing Objectives

Once jobs are defined, it is possible to develop training objectives. The training objective is the most important component in any training process. Clearly defined objectives are necessary in order to know what the end results of training must be in order to be effective. The *Trainer's Handbook: The AMA Guide to Effective Training* points out that the objective is not so much a statement of desired results, as a map of how to achieve those results. [5] Components of the training objective are: (1) description of the skills the trainees will need; (2) description of those skills as they relate to the working conditions; (3) detailed criteria to be met or other explanation of how the trainees will be evaluated; and (4) realistic expectations. [6]

With needs clearly defined, how will they be obtained? Objectives will decide what is taught and how. Knowledge of objectives will also give a sense of priorities. What must be learned first? At 8:00 A.M. Monday, when the doors of the library open for the first time during a semester or school year, what must the students assistants be ready to do? What needs to be done first?

Rules and Regulations

Each organization has a number of rules and regulations that students must follow. Some of these are dictated by the central hiring authority, some by the payroll office, and yet others by the individual area in which a student works. In all work situations, students will be expected to follow these "guidelines," and often will be evaluated on how well they perform. It is not fair to expect the students to remember a complex set of rules or guidelines without first providing something in writing, and going over what is given so that clarification can be made.

Guidelines for student behavior while on the job should be firm, yet not punitive. It is hoped that students will enjoy their work and that they will learn about their individual areas and the library in general. In addition, since librarians are training students to be excellent future employees, it is hoped that they will leave the library with a well-defined work ethic.

The following items should be included in a basic list of rules and regulations. Each organization will have additional specific items.

> An attendance policy should be clearly stated. This should also include time clock procedures. Rules regarding absences and substitutions need to be addressed as well.

> If students are expected to call in to report sickness or other emergency situations, they should be told when and where to call.

> The dress code should be covered. If shorts are not acceptable under any circumstances, let the students know ahead of time.

> Behavior while on the job can be included in these guidelines. Such items as: (1) do not encourage friends to visit; (2) no eating, drinking, or smoking; (3) how to avoid theft of belongings and office materials; (4) verbal etiquette; and (5) office responsibilities.

Developing Training Checklists

After the development of job descriptions, job objectives, and departmental rules and regulations, training checklists can be written. Training checklists state each area a student must be trained in to fulfill the objectives set for each position and to meet library standards. In listing each training need for each job, be sure that nothing will be missed during the training process, that the training process will follow in a logical sequence, that each position does not entail too much for one person to learn, and that the student is made aware of the rules.

Training checklists are usually one of two types. A simple checklist notes each area an employee must be trained in and, as the employee is trained, the item is simply checked off and the next item is then covered. An evaluative checklist gives the trainer the opportunity to note how the employee appears to be absorbing the information, and whether or not follow up is necessary. Both checklists give the employer an opportunity to quickly see where each employee is in the training process and, if necessary, who has been trained to do an assignment when a special occasion may occur. (See figures 2 and 3.)

Hiring Student Workers

With a clear analysis of departmental functions and an idea of the jobs to be done, the time has come to determine the student workforce. Hiring the right number of students is critical, and can only be determined by reviewing the workflow situation and available supervisory staff. Hiring more students than can be adequately trained and managed will create serious problems. Given the workforce available, try to hire exactly enough students to do the job. A small, well-trained workforce is preferable to many students unable to adequately carry out their duties. The key is that students be well trained and motivated. Both of these are benefits of highly structured training programs. A final suggestion is to be selective. Follow selection guidelines established for the tasks to be accomplished. Remember, for students to be well trained, there must be some reasonable expectation that the training can be accomplished. Select students who can be appropriately placed in the jobs.

A first step in knowing what kinds of student workers might be available is found in the application form. What attributes are important? Experience, background, interests, skills, and goals information can all provide a first look at the pool of prospective workers and determine where they could fit into the organization. Application information will also provide a basis for the interview process and help determine the direction of questioning for each interviewee. An application form will also provide the hours of availability so that the library knows who is available to perform the necessary tasks when they need to be done. (See figure 4.)

A second step is the interview process. Beach notes that there are three basic reasons for an interview. The interviewer is seeking sufficient information about the interviewee to be able to determine if he or she could fit into the organizational structure and, if so, what would be the most effective location.

Collection Maintenance Department

Orientation Checklist

Name _____   Date _____

Category: _____ Full time _____   Part time _____

I. Audiovisual Presentation _____

II. Building Tour _____

    A. Fire Extinguisher Demonstration _____

    B. Emergency Stairways _____

        1. West _____

        2. Southeast _____

    C. 4th Floor _____

        1. Textbook Room _____

        2. Group Study Rooms _____

    D. 3rd Floor and Mezzanine _____

        1. 3m Stacks _____

        2. 3rd Stacks _____

        3. Library Media Center _____

        4. Archives _____

    E. 2nd Floor and Mezzanine _____

        1. 2m Stacks _____

        2. 2nd Stacks _____

        3. Bargman Room _____

    F. First Floor _____

        1. Lobby _____

        2. Reference _____

        3. Microform _____

        4. Luis Terminals _____

        5. Circulation Desk _____

Fig. 2. Sample orientation checklist. This department-specific orientation checklist may be used to familiarize a new employee with the library and its operations. Printed by courtesy of the University of Detroit, McNichols Campus Library.

   6. Time Clock Room _____

   7. Technical Services _____

        a. Collection Maintenance _____

        b. Acquisitions/Receiving _____

        c. Cataloging _____

   8. Director's Office _____

   9. Conference room _____

   10. Staff Lounge _____

G. Basement _____

        1. Government Documents _____

        2. Thesis Room _____

        3. Basement Stacks _____

        4. Student or Patron Lounge _____

        5. Vending Machines _____

H. Off-site Storage (Arch. Bldg.) _____

III. Department Duties _____   Summary Sheet _____

   A. Department Organizaton _____

   B. Stacks and Special Collections _____

        1. Shelving _____

        2. Stack Maintenance _____

        3. Shifting _____

   C. Bargman Room _____

        1. Architecture Collection _____

        2. Current Periodical and Newspaper Collection _____

   D. Search _____

   E. Maintenance Reports _____

   F. Recordkeeping and Statistics _____

Fig. 2 continued.

Collection Maintenance Department

Training Checklist

Name _____   Hire Date _____

Department: Collection Maintenance _____

                    Other (specify) _____

Manuals issued: General Rules and Info.   _____

                    Department Rules and Info.   _____

                    Call Number Rules and Info.   _____

I. Introduction

    A. Demonstration _____

        1. Shelving _____

        2. Shelfreading _____

        3. Shifting _____

        4. Luis Demo _____

    B. Work with Experienced Student _____

II. General Training

    A. Written Call Number Test (Attach Results) _____

    B. Recorded Shelving—Regular Collection (Attach Results)

    Stack Level and Special Collection   Date

    3m

    3rd

    2m

    2nd

    Bsmt

Fig. 3. Sample training checklist. Example of a work area-specific training checklist. Note the very specific information that will be covered. Printed by courtesy of University of Detroit, McNichols Campus Library.

C. Recorded Shelving—Special Collections

Collection/Location   Date

Textbooks (4th)

Junior Literature (3m)

Current Periodicals (Bargman)

Current Newspapers (Bargman)

Theses and Dissertations (Bsmt)

D. Recorded Shelfreading

Floor   Date

E. Written Exercise (Attach Results) _____

F. Luis Exercise _____

G. Stack Maintenance _____

H. Assistance/Public Service to Patrons _____

III. Additional Training

A. Opening Procedures _____

1. Opening of Building _____

2. Carrel Clearing _____

3. Emptying of Trucks _____

B. Closing Procedures _____

1. Bargman Room Activities _____

2. Closing of Building _____

C. Cleaning _____

1. Supply Locations _____

2. Procedures and Techniques _____

IV. Bargman Room Training _____

A. Sorting and Shelving _____

1. Gathering items—First Floor _____

Fig. 3 continued.

2. Gathering Items—Bargman Room _____

3. Sorting _____

4. Shelving _____

B. Completed Volumes _____

1. Recognition and Exceptions _____

2. Removal from Shelf _____

3. Transport to Bindery Prep Shelf _____

C. Architecture Area—See Stacks Training _____

D. Shelfreading and Stack Maintenance _____

E. Current Newspaper Maintenance _____

V. Other Training

A. Computer Training _____

1. IBM Tutorial _____

2. WordPerfect _____

3. Lotus 123 _____

4. Excel _____

5. Other (specify) _____

B. Statistics and Lists _____

1. Shifting _____

2. Search _____

3. Other _____

C. Search _____

D. Other _____

Fig. 3 continued.

Seniority Date _____

Total Sem. Worked _____

Termination Dates _____ _____

Rehire Dates _____ _____

Name _____

Acct. _____

Unit _____

Pay Rate _____

Account/Pay Change _____

Eastern Michigan University

Learning Resources and Technologies

Student Employee Application

Date: _____

1. Name: _____ Soc. Sec. No.: _____

2. Local Address: _____ Phone: _____

3. Home Address: _____ Phone: _____

4. Current Status:

_____ EMU student, currently registered student # _____

_____ EMU student, not currently registered

5. Present year in school _____ Anticipated graduation date: _____

6. G.P.A. _____ Curriculum _____

7. Semesters you will be attending classes:

_____ Fall   _____ Winter   _____ Spring   _____ Summer

8. Unmet Need $ _____

9. Do you have a Work-Study grant? _____ Yes _____ No. If yes, you must bring us

your Work-Study card from the Student Employment Office. Amount of grant: $ _____

10. Are you presently employed by another EMU department? _____ Yes _____ No.

If yes, what department and how many hours per week? _____

11. List your previous work experience (most recent first):

Employer	Type of job	Dates Worked	Supervisor	Phone #
_____	_____	_____	_____	_____
_____	_____	_____	_____	_____

Fig. 4. Sample student employee application. A student employee application form may be as general or specific as is needed.

General Library

_____ *Circulation*—No prior experience needed. Weekends or evenings may be required.

_____ *Technical Services/Public Services*—May require computer skill or prior clerical background.

_____ *Copy Center*—No prior experience needed. Weekends or evenings may be required.

Instructional Support Center

_____ *Tutors*

_____ *Lab Assistants*

Media Services

_____ *Technical Assistant*—Good driving record required.

_____ *Media Assistant*—Some clerical background required.

12. Please answer the following questions completely, but in a concise manner:

a. What skills or previous job-related experience do you possess that would be beneficial to the LR&T?

b. Do you regularly use the library building?

c. Do you type? _____ Speed _____

d. Computer knowledge _____

e. Other office machines _____

Signature: _____ Date: _____

For Office Use Only

Position	Date Hired	Pay Rate	Supervisor's Initials
_____	_____	_____	_____
_____	_____	_____	_____

Fig. 4 continued.

The interviewee should be given sufficient information about the organization so that he or she might be able to determine what the job position might be, how it fits into the organizational operations, what would be required, and if he or she could fit in. And, finally, an interview must convey a positive image of the organization and its operations. The fact that this person is there for an interview is an indication that he or she will be a user of the facilities. An interview provides an excellent opportunity to present the organization in its clearest form, so that even if the person is not hired, he or she will still feel good and speak well of the institution.[7]

Although interviews cannot provide everything a supervisor needs to know about a perspective student worker, they do have a positive and significant predictive value. This is especially true if the interviewer is knowledgeable of the job positions being offered and of the departmental operations and can comfortably and truthfully answer any questions asked.

Beach classifies interviews into four basic types: (1) a planned interview, depth or action interview; (2) a patterned or standardized interview; (3) a stress or interrogative interview; and (4) an interview based on an examining board or panel.[8] Both the patterned and the stress interview are highly structured, with extremely comprehensive questions, and an overwhelming and somewhat threatening approach. With the built-in transiency and the beginning nature of a student assistant's employment, neither approach has applicability in this hiring process.

A planned interview outlines in advance the subject areas that need to be covered. The main objective of this type of interview is to get the interviewees to talk freely about themselves, especially on a social and personal level. Given the fact that most student assistants are inexperienced in the work area, librarians must rely more heavily on knowing what type of person a prospective student assistant might be. What are the person's likes, dislikes, hobbies, and interests? What are his or her recreational activities? What organizations is the student involved in? Such information may provide the only clues as to the suitability of student applicants. It is also important, in this type of interview, to be specific about the type of organization and the nature of the job and area being staffed.

The other type of interview that may be used is the examining board. This form of interview, completed by three or more persons, allows for a more comprehensive selection process while limiting biases and impressions that may develop in a one-person interview. Other than the fact that a potential student worker may feel more uncomfortable with more than one person as an interviewer, this type of interview is effective, efficient, and can be wisely used.

During the interview itself, simple interview guidelines should be followed. Use standardized, predesigned job related questions to insure that comparable information is obtained about each candidate, and be sure that all necessary information areas are covered. Keep the interviewee talking while you listen; a good rule to follow is that the interviewer should do no more than twenty percent of the talking. Probe to get complete information. Use open-ended questions that require more than a "yes" or "no" answer. Allow the candidate to elaborate through mirroring the conversation. Phrase questions with: How did . . . ; Why did you . . . ; Tell me (about your hobbies, the subjects you like best, least, etc.). [9]

Use hypothetical or actual past situations to assess knowledge, reactions, or understanding. This process may be used to assess the student's ability to deal with problem patrons, cultural differences, or to use critical thinking skills. Do not decide prematurely about a candidate's qualifications or abilities. Allow yourself and the candidate the full interview time to analyze his or her abilities and background.

Look for leadership experience. Help the interviewees note their achievements and discuss their assets. Use double-edged questions to discover what the student has learned about his or her strengths and weaknesses.

Try to determine what the student is looking for in a job. If the student has been previously employed, note progress from job to job. Look for any increase in responsibility, or for positions that gave special attention to hard work, including long hours or heavy labor. Note any jobs held for which the student may have been overqualified. Ask yourself if more responsibility could have been handled.

Discuss with the interviewee his or her previous education, and try to determine the current level of social adjustment. (References to homesickness are not a good sign.) In previous educational experiences, what subjects were best liked? What subjects were least liked? How does the student perform in school, based on grades? Watch for signs of ability and motivation. Take note of extracurricular activities, both in previous and current educational experiences. If there are few or no extracurricular activities, the student may be shy, introverted, inhibited, or may lack motivation. Participation often shows social development, including being comfortable with others the same age. If the student has participated in sports, he or she may have developed some competitive spirit, learned cooperation or teamwork. All of these attributes are useful for student library assistants before starting work in the library. (See figures 5 to 7.)

Testing Student Workers

A final part of the hiring decision can be a test of skills administered to the student applicant, either at the time of application or at the time of the interview. These tests of skills can be general in nature and can measure basic library knowledge. Whether or not to use a test must be decided by each individual library. When making this decision, consider the following:

> Will the information, skills, or abilities being tested be a part of the student assistant job?
> Will the student assistant need to know the information being tested, or be able to demonstrate the specific skill before being hired, or will this be part of the training program?
> Will test results be used to determine the training program?
> Will test results be used to justify not hiring a student who performs poorly?
> Will test results be used to place students in specific jobs or areas of the library?

Before determining that tests will be part of the process, it is wise to determine not only why they would be given, but also how the results will be used. It may be that students who score above a certain percentage would have basic skills and abilities and be able to function adequately in any library area. Others scoring below a particular percentage might be referred to other locations for employment. In order to make this kind of determination, however, several factors should be considered. It is possible that some students would perform poorly on a test (through test anxiety or pressure) but be able to function adequately within the library. Others, going into various locations (media or computer lab) may have skills and abilities not easily measured on a basic test, yet important for those other areas. These skills may be reported on the application, or be communicated during the interview. If, however, a student scored below the acceptable level, he or she might be denied employment.

In the current state of automated systems, it may be increasingly difficult to develop a meaningful test. Some students may come with a basic background in automation, others may not.

Interview Checklist

Name: Date:

Education:	Elementary	High School	College	Subject
School				
Dates				
Degrees				

Impressions:		Poor	Good	Excellent
Friendly				
Good with Public				
Speaking Skills				
Reading Skills				
Socialization				
Interest in Job				

Skills:

    ___Typing   ___Computer
    ___Calculator   ___IBM
    ___Filing   ___MAC
    ___Telephone   ___Other _____
    ___Languages _____

Experience:	Duties	Advancement	Reason for Leaving
Position			
Position			

Comments/Summary:

Interviewer:

Fig. 5. Sample interview checklist. An interview checklist provides a complete information list that can be arranged and checked off as needed.

Interview Outline

Name: _____ Date: _____

Education

Grades: _____

Best Subjects: _____

Worst Subjects: _____

Favorite Subject: _____

Social Activities: _____

Sports: _____

Awards: _____

Other: _____

Experience

Where: _____

Duties: _____

Best Part: _____

Worst Part: _____

Advancement: _____

Other: _____

Social

Current Activities: _____

Interests: _____

What Are They Looking For?

Experience: _____

Management Activities: _____

Money: _____

Socialization: _____

Other: _____

Summary/Recommendation

Interviewer: _____

Fig. 6. Sample interview outline. This generic interview guide details information that should be covered in most interviews; the format is especially useful when interviewing for many positions at one time.

Interview Review

Name: _____ Date: _____

Position: _____

_____

Education: _____

_____

_____

Training:

Experience:

Social Activities:

Personality:

Summary:

Recommendation: _____

_____

_____

Interviewer: _____

Fig. 7. Sample interview review. This format allows the interviewer to summarize responses openly or note specific information applicable to a particular position.

With the automated systems taking over more of the "technical" jobs, such as filing, it is less likely that students will have a basic background in filing rules. They may have little more than knowledge of the alphabet. Aptitude for automated services may be a comparable substitute for other types of tests.

Those being hired for shelving may or may not have basic knowledge of the classification system. However, students who display organizational and analytical skills should be able to learn the shelving system with proper training. Making a determination of those skills during the interview and from information on the application could be sufficient for the hiring decision.

Tests may be useful in determining if students are capable of understanding basic written English. Foreign students who do not have sufficient command of the language to pass a basic test might not do well in some library jobs. Even though they may be able to learn the functions of the library, understanding written instructions and information will be critical.

If tests of basic skills and abilities are used, they should be carefully correlated with the application and interview. Additional information about the student's skills should be collected and used before determining final hiring and placement.

Planning the Program

Carefully planning and organizing the training process is essential if the program is to function appropriately. Planning the program requires knowledge of both the essentials of the job(s) to be included and of the teaching and learning processes. What can be done to enhance, rather than inhibit, student learning?

Before the actual development of the various components and lessons, it is helpful to develop some standards for the training program as a whole. Previously defined objectives should be incorporated into each component of the program. The training checklist for each area should be reviewed so that no important element of the job is left out.

The training methods, as well as the content, must be determined ahead of time. All materials should be developed well in advance. The methods and materials must take into account that all learners do not learn in the same way or at the same pace. It is important that a variety of methods and tools be used during the entire process. A well-planned, carefully organized program will integrate this variety in a cohesive manner, fitting in each type of training or using each tool where it fits best.

While many classroom teachers are adept at using a variety of teaching methods and tools (such as small group discussion groups and overhead projectors), often librarians have not had the opportunity to become familiar with them. Therefore, it may be helpful to review some training tools and methods that may be used in a variety of ways to enhance the training (learning) process.

Training Tools and Methods

Numerous training tools and methods that can be used in most work situations are readily available. All tools and methods should be adapted to each job so that maximum benefit and use many be derived for both the supervisor and the student assistant.

The following training tools and methods, their "pros" and "cons" of usage, are offered as possible components of any training program.

Manuals

Manuals used for training may be of two types: a manual to read, giving guidelines and procedures for specific tasks, or a manual in a workbook format that the trainee first fills out and then is reviewed by the supervisor.

One specific thought should be kept in mind when using or developing a training manual—reading ability. Reading ability has been found to relate directly to job proficiency. In the article "Maybe They Can't Read the Manual," it is noted that some training manuals are just too hard for some trainees to read.[10] Consider the various backgrounds of the prospective student workers, including cultural diversity and the various ways that people learn. To depend completely on a training manual limits the ability of some students to learn well. Some people learn better by listening, doing, observing, etc. A manual is useful as a training tool if other methods are also used in order to give the trainee every opportunity to learn. A manual should always be made available for the student to refer back to when necessary, or as a review.

Handouts

Handouts on specific procedures are useful training aids for workers, and are also a good way to provide extra information to someone having difficulty. If student assistants are provided with either a folder or a specific area for placement of information, a handout becomes an excellent means of providing information of a new process or procedure. Keep in mind, however, the variances in reading ability and understanding. Handouts may be used as an additional tool for reference after the assistant has been shown a specific job area or has heard a new process explained.

Postings

Posting information in an outline format is a good way for providing quick information or guidelines either at the point of reference or on a bulletin board. To provide a student worker with information on the various types of identification and the checkout rules that apply at the point of check out allows them to verify what is correct or update them on a little-used patron category. Posted information should not be in a lengthy narrative format, but rather one that can be quickly read. Posted information may also be used to notify student assistants of problems in certain areas (requesting all students reread a particular part of the manual), or used to remind them to ask for additional information if they are not clear on a particular task.

Lecture

A classroom lecture is one of the best ways to convey information to a group. Two problems that might occur are getting everyone together at the same time (who is working the front counter?) and the different learning levels of a diverse group of students. How does the trainer know that everyone is understanding a particular procedure? Most student assistants are hesitant to admit a lack of comprehension, especially if they think everyone else understands. As with job design, if a lecture is too simplistic for the majority, they will lose interest and not pay attention; If it is too difficult, students will not grasp important guidelines and processes. A good rule to follow is that college graduates will pay attention for thirty minutes; high school graduates, fifteen to twenty minutes; high school level and below, ten minutes or less. [11] A lecture needs to be very specific, covering only two or three points at a time. A useful lecture tool is to provide student handouts during the lecture, to follow or to read later. Remember, know the group.

Workshops

A workshop is an effective training tool because it combines both the lecture format with participation by the group. A workshop is not as passive as a lecture. Student assistants are more actively involved and will tend to learn from one another as ideas and experiences are tossed about. Again, it is difficult to find a time to bring this group together, and there will always be those who might shy away from active participation.

Case Study

Case studies in training are an extension of workshops. Case studies are generally conducted in a workshop atmosphere, and students quickly learn that there is usually more than one way to approach a given situation. This method provides student assistants with background in facing problem situations since the cases are based upon actual experiences that occurred in the department; it also provides an opportunity to develop analytical thinking and problem-solving abilities. This method also tends to reduce any narrow-minded structures a student may have developed in the past. Case studies can be used in training on a one-to-one basis, and also in a classroom situation. Cases must be developed by the supervisors. While they must be realistic, students should not be able to connect the case situation to any particular employee or student assistant.

Programmed Instruction

Programmed instruction allows a trainee to learn at his or her own pace and provides the learner with active participation at each step. This tool is excellent in teaching job routines, especially when dealing with a diversity of backgrounds and cultures. The supervisor can tell at each level of learning whether or not the trainee has grasped the basic job knowledge or if additional training or a change in job positions is indicated. Because each job routine is broken down into small stages for learning, it is easy to note any particular learning abilities of the trainee and where they might be best utilized. This tool is time consuming to develop and process in a training program, but can be used in addition to more traditional methods or as an option for additional training in special situations. Programmed instruction can be either used with paper and pencil or computers (see below).

Computer-Assisted Instruction

In the "high-tech" arena of electronic technologies, the computer and the somewhat newer combination of computer and video (interactive video) are the two most promising candidates for appropriate use in the training of student assistants.

Computer-assisted instruction is similar to programmed instruction because students move at their own pace and the trainer knows in what areas they may be having difficulties. An excellent tool for drill and practice, it is very expensive to develop but it is durable in most library situations. For the most part, library supervisors will not want to develop their own programs unless they are willing to spend a great deal of time. Good CAI programs require knowledge of instructional design principles as well as knowledge of the computer. Packages are now available that help alleviate some computer time involved.

Standard computer use in bibliographic instruction has been going on for many years. A good reference source for such computer-assisted-instruction software is the LOEX Clearinghouse. However, the main problem with the more traditional CAI software is that either the trainer must use exact copies of the software (with permission of the developer) or have someone with programming skills adapt existing software or develop new software. Since most training programs need to be library-specific, this limitation has been a serious barrier to the effective use of CAI in training. The only exception to the standard computer-based rule is in the area of automated library systems. For example, it is possible to build in training modules to the NOTIS library system. Once again, the LOEX Clearinghouse is a good reference source because it has just been named the official depository for instruction materials on NOTIS. If the library has a different automated system, it will want to check with the vendor to see what training options are available within the system.

A new development in the world of personal computers has opened up a much more viable opportunity for appropriate computer use in student assistant training. This is the introduction of what is generically known as hypertext. The most frequently used adaptation of hypertext today is Apple Computer's MacIntosh hypermedia. With very little training, an individual can use this icon-based system to create programs of instruction that include quite sophisticated graphics as well as text. In order to adapt or develop hypermedia software, the individual does not need a background in computer language programming. He or she still needs to have a basic knowledge of computing and the appropriate instructional development strategies, but most of the "high-tech" mystery has been taken out of the actual program creation and use.

Another very recent alternative is IBM's Windows. This new alternative gives MS-DOS users and IBM devotees a chance at using a hypertext world that up to now has been the exclusive domain of Apple's hypermedia.

Incidentally, as this book is being completed, the pricing structures for both MacIntosh and IBM equipment are becoming more affordable for the institutional user. The development units are still in the $1,000 to $3,000 range; however, the student models are now less than $1,000 for the first time.

Hypertext (either hypermedia or Windows) has brought computer-assisted training into the realm of possibility for library student assistant training applications. This graphic (non-video) based software application can be used today, and for most applications the excellent graphics are very sufficient for all training needs. Apple, IBM, or the many clone vendors will be most happy to present the details of their hypertext applications.

In order to effectively use CAI, it must be remembered that computers must be easily accessible for student assistants to use.

Role Playing and Simulations

Role playing, in which two or more students are put in a practice situation and pretend that the situation is real, is used primarily to give trainees an opportunity to learn human relation skills through practice and to give them an insight into their own reactions, views, and behaviors. Role playing can be used in a classroom situation or on a one-to-one basis. Phone procedures and handling problem patrons are two training areas where role playing will make the student feel more at ease when placed in a real situation.

Simulation techniques, similar to role playing, can also be useful tools in training student assistance. A student can be prepared for daily operations and unpleasant situations. Simulations require that the situation to be learned be reproduced exactly, including all equipment. The time and expense of developing this type of training tool is often not in the budget of most libraries and can often be substituted by role-playing activities.

Audiovisual Aids

The use of audiovisual aids in training can provide an added component to learning. Through the use of such aids, training can be varied enough to give all students the opportunity to learn through their preferred styles. In addition, audiovisual aids often add spice to presentations, making them more interesting. They can easily focus attention on the topic at hand. While constant use of these aids is not recommended, they can be useful in some library training situations.

Audiovisual aids present unique requirements. They can be used with either a small or large group of students, or can be set up in an individual training station for students to view independently. Since it is often difficult to gather even a small group of students more than a few times, the use of this equipment for groups will be saved for special times. If the equipment is left for individual viewing, a room must be designated for that purpose, and some meaningful preliminary instruction must take place so that the context in which the material is being viewed is clear.

Slides add an interesting dimension to some aspects of training. They can be used to "take students where they can not go" by bringing pictures of places and activities to them. With the necessary equipment available, slides are easy to produce and relatively easy to use. Using a copy stand, slides can be made of charts, graphs, or pictures from books. Bringing a camera to work and taking a few "live" pictures can provide students an introduction to places and people before they actually see them. A slide presentation can be easily updated by replacing outdated slides with new ones, without changing the entire program.

An excellent individualized training device is the *slide/tape presentation*. Adding synchronized audiotape to a slide presentation and running the presentation on a slide/tape player allows students to view an entire training session individually. Students can go at a comfortable pace when viewing, and can both see and hear information. This type of program requires the making of an audiotape for the slide presentation and synchronizing the tape with the appropriate slides. Changing the program becomes a little more difficult if the tape must be changed, but new pictures can be added at any time.

Audiotapes can be used without slides but are somewhat limited. Students are accustomed to being able to see action while hearing voices and may not focus attention on this medium.

Flipcharts are versatile in training uses, can be quickly adapted to changes, and most people feel comfortable with them. Most trainers develop either a love or hate relationship with the use of flipcharts in training. As the classic article "Dead Men Don't Use Flipcharts" stated, "the humble flipchart stands ready in its elegant simplicity to meet and exceed the demand of absolutely any instructional situation." [12] One thing to keep in mind is that the charts must be visible to everyone, as they are generally used as part of a lecture in a group setting.

Overhead projectors project images onto a large screen and can be used in three ways. First, charts, graphs, instructions or other written material can be made into transparencies in a formal program to supplement lecture material. These can be made from drawings, books, or computer printouts. Second, write-on acetate can be used with special transparency pens and can substitute for a chalk board or flipchart. The instructor can emphasize specific points while lecturing and students can easily take notes. Third, the overhead projector can be used in conjunction with an *LCD computer projection device* to project the output from a computer terminal onto the screen. This is particularly helpful in training sessions with automated library services. Many times it is not feasible for each student in a group session to have a terminal, but all students can see live transactions happening when projected onto a large screen.

Overhead projectors and computer projection devices are best used in group situations. This again requires a classroom situation for the training.

Films have significant applicability in training. Many commercially produced training films are available for purchase or rental and can provide excellent action orientation to students. On film, simulated situations can provide students with a taste of the real situation in the workplace. Usually 16mm films must be shown in a darkened room, again requiring a classroom or other appropriate space.

Purchasing or renting films for student assistant training can be an expensive route. Good films are expensive, and can usually be used only once with each group. Before purchasing a film, preview it to be certain it meets the training objectives.

"Video is probably the most dynamic and exciting invention for training since the overhead projector." [13] It provides the ease of slides and the action of film without the difficulties of either. Commercially prepared videotapes are expensive to rent or purchase, but with a video camera, it is possible to make videos on site using real student assistants in "real" (or simulated) situations. Videotapes are reusable, can be changed or updated easily, and can be watched as easily individually as in large groups.

Videotaping students while they practice what they have learned gives them immediate feedback on their performance. Student assistants can both watch others performing and watch themselves.

The newest form of high-tech electronic technology is known generically as Interactive Video. Various vendors have chosen specific labels for this combination of computer and video technologies; however, in order to use interactive video, one will need a computer (with authoring software or hypertext), a video device (tape, videodisc, or CD-ROM disc), and an interface device. The computer and video player are hooked together so that the student can use both devices at once. Using a computer program, the video is played when appropriate to the information being presented. The computer program can also generate questions or problems or other instructional sequences for the student to work on. Using interactive video, students can be presented with instructional video segments, answer questions on the computer about the segments, and be directed to additional training depending on the answers which have been selected.

The obvious attraction to this multimedia approach to training is that it allows for the combination of a variety of media: high-quality sound, text, motion video, still frames, graphics, and music. Further, a trainer can effectively present information and engage students in a full-sensory learning environment. The student can explore a multimedia presentation according to his or her own level, need, and learning style. This type of technology-assisted training allows for interaction between the student and the training system; the learning becomes more intuitive, more spontaneous, and, in fact, more fun.

Use of interactive video requires that a computer and a video playback unit be reserved for this purpose. Videotape has been used, but it cumbersome to access and is not of high quality. Videodisc provides ease of access, excellent still-frame pictures as well as full-motion video, and high quality. However, it has two basic drawbacks for widespread use in library student assistant training. They are cost and cost. First, the cost of the dedicated interactive video system itself is prohibitive for most libraries (between $8,000 and $10,000 each). Second, the cost of developing library-specific programs is also prohibitive for most libraries. Even with the use of less-expensive videotape, each video sequence must be locally produced. If videodiscs are used, they have to be produced and mastered (at a minimum cost of $1,500 each), and the video images cannot be changed or updated without mastering a new videodisc. Also, the availability of qualified staff to produce these more sophisticated programs is a limiting factor for most libraries at this time. Perhaps in time this newest electronic technology will become more accessible to training applications such as those in libraries.

In the future we may see a simplified (and inexpensive as well) work station that will foster easy creation of multimedia programs by library staff and their use by student assistants.

All training tools and methods are useful additions to student assistant training when used in conjunction with training objectives. All student learning styles can be accommodated when a variety of types of tools and methods is used.

**Evaluating Student
Workers**

Employment evaluations can be an effective management tool. Evaluations not only assist employees in knowing where they stand in the organization, but may also aid them in developing better work habits, improving public relations skills, and giving them a general perspective on what type of job or profession they may want to pursue as adults. For the organization, job evaluations are a valuable asset in the design of training programs, in that they point out the weaknesses, strengths, and overall job design needs. As Robert D. Stueart states in *Library Management*, "If properly conducted, the performance evaluation will give every level of management a better understanding of the individuals capabilities and potential with the organization . . . . The performance evaluation process should help employees establish personal goals that will enable them to grow and develop and that will further implement the institutional goals." [14]

Performance evaluations for the employee may be on two levels: during employment, and at the end of employment. Evaluation in the form of tests during employment allows the supervisor to quickly note where an employee may be misunderstanding a process or guideline before the application of incorrect procedures become a large problem. Also, if a majority of the workforce is misguided, there is a significant implication that something is wrong in the training process. Many people have "test phobia," so it is important that the students know the purpose of any testing that is to be done, that it is a review process to see where they—and their trainers—stand in work performance and operations, and that nothing punitive will come out of the results. If there is a major problem with the work of student assistants within an area, a testing evaluation is an excellent way of pinpointing where the problem originates and gives the supervisor an indirect approach in tutoring the student assistant in correcting the problem.

Evaluation at the end of employment, or at a significant ending phase of employment (end of semester or school year) is another effective way of assisting both the employee and the training process. This format of performance appraisal is somewhat on the more personal level but of no less value for the training process evaluation. An employee's performance should be measured against the standards stated in the job description, objectives, and job design. Not only is this evaluation necessary for future promotions, pay increases, and increases in responsibility, but it is also imperative for legal purposes in the process of terminating an employee. This form of evaluation is usually on a rating scale: poor - - - - - superior, or on a scale of 1 - - - - - 5, and rates the employee's attitude, responsibility, public service skills, and attendance. (See figures 8 and 9.)

Stueart goes on to state that the standards that need to be established in the design of performance evaluations fall into three areas: quality-quantity standards; desired effect standards; and manner of performance standards.[15] How well does the employee perform the various tasks set forth in the job description, and how much of each task is actually accomplished; is the work complete, accurate, and performed on time, enhancing the goals and objectives of the institution and users; are sound data gathered as a basis for judgment and decisions; is the work accomplished in cooperation with others, without friction; can the employee adapt to new programs or processes?

Pitfalls to be aware of, as noted by the Denver Public Library's *Manual for Performance Evaluation*, are: the error of the halo effect—supervisors often evaluate the employee in terms of their personal mental attitude about the employee rather than by careful attention to the individual factors of work performance; the error of prejudice and partiality—an error in judgment and of the Constitution; the error of leniency, softness or spinelessness—taking the easy way out when a supervisor can't face the unpleasantness that may arise from an unfavorable evaluation; the error of the central tendency—a rating that is near the norm becomes a central tendency error if it does not reflect true performance; the error of contrast—is the rating the measure of the work that this employee has actually accomplished, or is it a measure of his or her potential; and the error of association—rating factors at the same degree because they follow each other on the page as a result of a tired, hurried, or bored evaluation.[16]

Whatever format an evaluation takes, whether it is in a question format during a working period or at the end of the employment, an important element must be feedback. An evaluation that is not reviewed with an employee, to tell him or her that the work is fine, or that the supervisor enjoyed having him or her as an employee but feels some areas might need work, is a wasted effort. An evaluation is a very important tool in the development of work habits and employment goals for the student assistant and no evaluation should be overlooked for its value.

Evaluations of the employee assist the organization in an on-going review of training methods and in the preliminary processes leading to the training program. Also, student employee evaluations of the job and the training make valuable contributions to the review process and to the training program design. What is the employee's interpretation of the training received?

Student Evaluation

Name: _____

Position: _____

Hire Date: _____   Current Date: _____

_____

Please rate on a scale from 1 to 5:   1 Poor → 5 Excellent

Work Quality: _____   Comment: _____

Work Quantity: _____   Comment: _____

Attendance: _____   Comment: _____

Attitude: _____   Comment: _____

Responsibility: _____   Comment: _____

_____

Please answer the following questions:

Is this student suited for this position? _____

Have this student's duties increased? _____

Have you been pleased with this student's overall performance? _____

Other comments: _____

_____

Evaluator: _____   Date: _____

Fig. 8. Sample student evaluation. This short evaluation can be used in all work areas. It could also be used as an intermediary review after a designated period of time or, with additional questions "Reason for termination" and "Would you rehire," could be used when employment is terminated. Variations of this form could include a rating scale, yes or no, more true than false, etc.

University Library

Learning Resources and Technologies

This employee appraisal form is used when a student assistant terminates service with the university library. It may be used to supplement a questionnaire for requested recommendations.

Name _____

Area of Assignment _____

Reason for Termination _____

Length of Service _____

Would you rehire? _____

Accuracy

_____ Above average   Comments:

_____ Average

_____ Below average

Thoroughness

_____ Above average

_____ Average

_____ Below average

Quality of work

_____ Above average

_____ Average

_____ Below average

Attendance

_____ Above average

_____ Average

_____ Below average

Appearance (grooming)

_____ Above average

_____ Average

_____ Below average

Courtesy and Tact

_____ Above average

_____ Average

_____ Below average

Cooperativeness

_____ Above average   Rating Supervisor _____

_____ Average   Position _____

_____ Below average   Date _____

Fig. 9. Sample employee appraisal.

Did the application form give both the employee and the supervisor sufficient information for the interview process? Did the interview provide the employee with a valid idea of what the job situation would be, what the expectations were, including hours to be worked? Did the interview process provide the supervisor with sufficient information for hiring the right person for the right job? Did the job analysis and work-flow design prove correct, or did the job descriptions not line up correctly to provide an even flow of work assignments? Is there sufficient motivation in each job to keep the employee interested, enthusiastic, etc., or does the employee evaluation show that workers were bored or underutilized? Evaluations of the employee and by the employee are a valuable management tool in reassessing and analyzing the best methods for training needs and demands. (See figure 10.)

A well-prepared, carefully planned training program requires a great deal of advance preparation in order to be successful. Much of the preparation comes before the actual development of a training outline. An added benefit of a new training program may be more clearly defined jobs, written job descriptions and clearly defined, written policies and procedures. These things are useful tools in any organization. Students and staff alike will appreciate the new structure.

The delivery of the actual training is as important as the preparation. Chapter 4 discusses the actual program and provides examples of training information.

Program Evaluation

To assist in improving the library's operation, please complete the following questionnaire and return it to _____ before you leave your current employment.

Library in General

1. What do you think the library does best?

2. What do you think the library could do better?

3. What do you like least about the library?

4. How do you think the library could better serve our patrons?

Other comments:

As an Assistant

1. What do you like best about your job?

2. What do you like least about your job?

3. Do you feel your library training was sufficient?

4. What more do you feel we should include in our training program?

5. Do you feel you are sufficiently supervised? Oversupervised? Undersupervised?

6. Is this job what you thought it would be? Better or worse?

Other comments:

Date: _____   Are you employed in a ____ Technical ____ Public ____ Special area?

Fig. 10. Sample program evaluation. This format is one option of providing the library with feedback on its operations. These same questions could be asked with a rating scale, checklist, or with very specific area related questions.

References

1. Dale S. Beach, *Personnel: The Management of People at Work*, 5th ed. (New York: Macmillan, 1985), p. 97.
2. Beach, pp. 97–101.
3. Charles Labelle with Susan Bookbinder et al., *Finding, Selecting, Developing and Retaining Data Processing Professionals Through Effective Human Resources Management* (New York: Van Nostrand Reinhold, 1983), p. 52.
4. Labelle, p. 165.
5. Gary Mitchell, *The Trainer's Handbook: The AMA Guide to Effective Training* (New York: AMACOM, 1987), p. 68.
6. Mitchell, p. 46.
7. Beach, p. 164.
8. Beach, p. 167.
9. Darrel R. Brown, "Sharpening Your Job Interviewing Techniques," *Supervisory Management* 30:29 (Aug. 1985).
10. "Maybe They Can't Read the Manual," *Training* 11:36–37 (June 1974).
11. Mitchell, p. 168.
12. "Dead Men Don't Use Flipcharts," *Training* 21:35–40 (Feb. 1984).
13. Mitchell, p. 238.
14. Robert D. Stueart and John Taylor Eastlick, *Library Management*, 2nd ed. (Littleton, Colo.: Libraries Unlimited, 1981), p. 97.
15. Stueart, p. 98.
16. Stueart, p. 98.

Chapter 4   The Training Program

Formal training sessions with all student employees present may take place once or twice near the beginning of a hiring period. Continued training, in small groups or one-on-one with either the supervisor or a peer, may take place during the first several weeks of the session. In order to accommodate all training in an organized manner, the following helpful hints are offered.

Schedule at least one session for all student assistants at which they are introduced to all staff, including the administrators, and to each other. Students need to become acquainted with their coworkers so that they can begin to work together as a team; this will also make it easier for students to arrange for subbing assigments. Many lasting friendships are started through interaction at work. The "team meeting" helps build camaraderie.

Provide each student with a folder or an area (such as a cubbyhole) in which he or she is expected to keep all important written materials, such as a job description, training checklists, or any current written communication from the supervisor. All student folders should be filed at a central location. Students should leave these folders at work and check them daily. They can be used as a private communication device between supervisor and student, between student and student, as well as a general avenue of communication for all students.

Each student should be given a training checklist to be kept in his or her folder or cubbyhole. The checklist is to be with the student anytime training is taking place. (The exact checklist would be dependent upon the area of the library to which the student is assigned.) The checklist is especially valuable for one-on-one and peer training sessions. Those doing the training will know exactly where to start and what yet needs to be covered. There is no guess work. The checklist is also a useful tool for supervisors who need to assign specific tasks to specific students. In case there is any question whether or not the student has been trained for that task, all supervisors can immediately check the list.

Provide each student with a written copy of the job description for his or her particular job. This should be kept in the individual's folder and can be referred to when doing the student evaluation, or at any time when questions or problems arise.

At the initial training session, provide each student with written guidelines as well as verbal instructions. The written guidelines should be kept in the folder for future reference. A list of some essentials follows:

> Where to go to get information you don't know, and who to go to for answers.
> An organizational chart of the library and of the university or larger organization.
> A list of employment responsibilities (sometimes called rules and regulations). Consider having students sign these to indicate they have read and understood them.
> A list of all administrators' names, job titles, and locations.
> Each student's individual copy of any basic library handout that patrons receive. Assistants should be aware of any patron information.
> A current copy of the complete student schedule.
> And, an opportunity to ask questions!

Other written items may be necessary for a particular situation. The folder is an excellent vehicle for distributing new information or updates. Students should be made aware that they will be held responsible for any information found in their folders.

Designate a bulletin board especially for student assistant communication. This bulletin board can be used by both supervisors and students to communicate with each other. Supervisors may want to make announcements about library hours or services, and students may wish to advertise for substitutes. A bulletin board may also be provided via a computer screen that everyone checks daily. This is an excellent way to introduce students to an advancing technology. Both types of bulletin boards are a good place for open communication exchange.

Provide students an opportunity to give feedback on the training program. Ask for their input and suggestions about what could be done better or differently. Keep this evaluation of the training short and to the point so that students will complete it and turn it in. Also, keep this anonymous.

Helpful Hints for Training Students

Make suggestions, don't give orders. As long as it doesn't really matter in what order a student completes a task, let the student decide what works best. What difference does it make whether the student stamps date dues as I do, four books then four cards, or as others may prefer, one book, one card? As long as the goal, to properly check out material, is met, the methods of achieving this goal can be as varied as the student assistants themselves. Suggest what might be done, but do not order it. Let the students feel comfortable with their work. Students will also react to the prospect that they have some say in how their work is accomplished. They can, in effect, determine their workflow. Giving students this kind of variation allows them to make their own decisions and raises self esteem.

Sell the job to the student on a personal level—"What's in it for me?" Design of the jobs and the training they receive should clearly indicate to students the benefits of library work. Skills learned as a library assistant can benefit the student now and later. In learning the system of book order processing, for example, the student will learn what new materials are now or are soon to be available. Also learned will be methods for determining correct authors and titles. Correct bibliographic information can be helpful for term papers, classwork, to help friends or relatives. In training, emphasize the ultimate benefit of the job to the student.

Define the necessary structures as regulations, not punitive measures. Help students understand *why* structures are in place. No one enjoys hearing " . . . because we've always done it that way" in response to why a procedure is followed. An understanding of the basis upon which structures are built goes a long way to increasing students' knowledge of the organization. In response to a student's question about why a valid identification card is required, explain the regulation indicating consequences of the nonreturn of borrowed materials with no current information. This would create difficulties for other patrons who might need the same information. By explaining to the student assistant that the regulation exists for a reason, and that reason benefits both the patrons and the library, some logical meaning is given to the structures.

Maintain a leadership role. Gain and maintain the students' respect. Always be sure that all student supervisors know the system. Anyone who trains and manages student assistants must be aware of policy changes, location changes, and other administrative moves. Those in charge must truly be in charge and know the answer to all questions or where to go for an answer to solve all problems. The buck stops here! It is also important that the students always know with whom the buck stops and feel that they will be supported when turning over problems that deserve supervisory response. A high level of student morale can only be maintained through consistent leadership and support.

A Training Model
Structural Context

Show students how they relate to the structure of the area they are being hired to staff. At this time also show them how they relate to the department, the library organization, the governing authorities, and the community. An organizational chart that shows students how they fit into the larger organization of the library helps give students a feeling that their small jobs are important within the larger context. If the chart clearly explains that the circulation department is only one department within the library but that its work affects other departments, such as reference and technical services, students may feel their jobs increase in importance (fig. 11). The organizational chart also can show that all departments come together through the central administration, and therefore affect the entire organization.

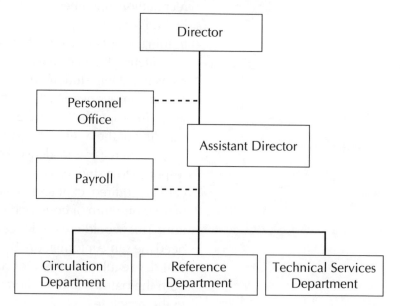

Fig. 11. Sample general organizational chart. This type of organizational chart can be used in most library situations with more specific verbal or written organization information provided.

If students are shown an organizational chart which explains the library's place within the university (or community), students can clearly see the part they play in the academic mission of the organization. For example, the library may be part of the academic or instructional division that reports to the provost or vice president. Seen in this way, the library's importance is emphasized. Student assistants, therefore, have a part to play in the overall mission, with the effect of their work extending beyond one building.

The key is to show them how they fit in, both through organizational charts and by making them aware of their value through their involvement with library happenings, noting any scheduled events in which they will be included.

Frame of Reference

Build a frame of reference for each employee to turn to and rely on. A frame of reference may be started with a tour of the building, during which not only areas are pointed out but also the persons in charge are introduced. This tour gives assistants a feel for the chain of command, lets them know who will answer questions, introduce the staff, and lets the employees meet the student assistants. A frame of reference should also be built with the availability of manuals or "cheat sheets" throughout an area for quick referrals.

Procedures

Written Procedures

Provide each student specific written procedures for his or her individual work area. (It can be a quick reference guide or how-to-do-it.) Also provide an opportunity to read the procedures manual. Students should read the manual in small chunks, not from cover to cover in one sitting. They should be encouraged to practice what they read after each section of the procedures manual.

It is important that students read as much about the entire unit as possible, since they must understand all that goes on in the unit and the rest of the building. Student assistants will invariably answer patron questions about other areas, or may have to direct patrons to other areas for services. Directing patrons to the wrong areas will cause patron frustration and result in poor service. Provide lists of service people, their telephone numbers and locations, and make these lists easily accessible to the assistants.

Critical Thinking   Instruct students in the fine art of asking questions. This will help them develop critical thinking and analysis skills, as well as giving them the capability of accurately determining what a patron really wants. Every public service staff person has been faced with the "detective game."

Students most often play twenty questions with the patron. Sometimes patrons know what they want but either don't know how to ask for it (calling transparencies films or slides, for example) or are embarrassed to have to ask someone for it. They may not know exactly what they want, as with a particular large piece of equipment or software package.

Provide students with a list of questions they might ask patrons to help determine, absolutely, what is needed. What is the problem? (The patron has asked at the reserve desk for a book. The student assistant asks the patron if the book is on reserve, and for what class. The patron doesn't know if it's on reserve or not.) The student assistant can quickly assess the problem, and can get more details about it by asking more questions. (The student might then state the problem: "You need the book, *The Closing of the American Mind*, which might be on reserve, but we don't know for sure.")

The student assistant then would know to go to step two in the critical thinking process: What are the alternatives? Determining whether the book is or is not on reserve could be done in several ways, and with further questioning it could be determined for what class the book might be on reserve, who the professor is, and what led the patron to believe that the book was on reserve. It could also be determined that the patron had or had not already checked to see if the book was in the general library collection.

Step three in the critical thinking process is to determine various alternatives, and to look at the advantages and disadvantages of each. The student assistant again could ask the patron questions to help determine what solutions might be feasible. The reference librarian is a possible alternative, if it's during reference hours, and if the librarian is not busy with an already long line of patrons. The catalog (card or online) is an alternative. Through additional questions it can be determined if this is a good option or not. Finally, the student assistant should reach step four, the solution. The patron would then either be given the book from reserve, find the call number, or seek help from the reference librarian. Through this entire process the student assistant is using critical thinking skills and good questioning techniques.

Service Orientation

Since libraries are service (or support) organizations, it is important that the service be inherent in all training. From the top down, library administrators must believe and act as though providing information access and service to library patrons is the primary reason for existence. In the written training materials, it is important that this philosophy be clearly stated. It is also necessary to actively stress customer relations through three critical service areas: (1) one-on-one; (2) on the telephone; and (3) in hostile (complaint) situations.

All students, whether they work directly in public services or in other areas, must be given instruction in customer (patron) service. Students may be asked questions, or may need to give directions or explanations, and will thus be acting as public service agents.

Patron service at the front line is one-on-one. An important aspect of good service is knowledge of the organization. Before beginning work with the public, students should have completed a review of the services available and their individual responsibilities so they know what can be done for the patrons. Knowledge of and competence in the operations gives students a powerful base from which to work. Providing written guides aids the student and gives patrons the assurance that they are being helped.

One-on-One Patron Service

Training in one-on-one patron service is a good time to make use of audiovisual materials or other training aids and to provide either written guidelines or a brochure. Some students will already have experience serving customers, especially if they have worked in fast food restaurants. Those students who have experience can be paired with new students who do not, to be certain that the "golden rules of good service" are discussed and understood.

For example, these rules should include such things as:

Please remember that to the patron, you are the library. We will all be judged by your actions. Therefore, do all you can to maintain a positive public image.

Service to the patrons is your first priority. Even though you should remain busy with library work, it is important that you are always ready to stop your work and serve the patron. If it is necessary that you finish what you are currently involved in, let the patron know that you are aware of his or her presence and will be available soon.

If you are sitting, either behind a counter or at a desk, get up and go to the patron. This assures the patron that you will be giving him or her undivided attention and that you are really interested in being of help.

Greet the patron with a smile. It is more likely that the encounter will be a pleasant one if it starts with a smile. Also remember to be polite.

Listen attentively to the patron's needs. Make mental or written notes of these needs so that you can service them without asking the patron to repeat the request. Ask appropriate questions to clarify the patron's needs. Provide paper and pencil at many locations.

Do what you can to satisfy the patron's needs or requests. Use your best judgment and your knowledge of the library procedures to give the best possible service.

Telephone Service

The telephone can be both a blessing and a curse; some days it seems the phone will never stop ringing. Students answering the phone must realize that it is also a part of the service component. Audiovisual materials are available that can be used to demonstrate proper telephone etiquette. Practice with telephones (simulation and role playing) is another excellent way to demonstrate and teach students how to handle telephone calls.

The following list is a sample of those items that students need to know and practice.

1. The telephone is an important business tool. Therefore, it is to be used for business purposes only. Do not make or receive personal calls while working. (Staff, as an example, shouldn't either.)

2. When it is your responsibility to answer the phone, try to answer it promptly, not later than the fourth ring. If necessary, indicate to the caller that you are busy and ask if he or she can please hold.

3. When answering the phone, identify the exact location (media, circulation, etc.) and offer to be of service. Example: "Library circulation, How may I help you?" Provide lists of office phone numbers near the phone so that students can quickly redirect a call. Teach students how to transfer calls.

4. Always have paper and pencil close; preferably the pencil will already be in hand. You may need to jot down items to remember, or take a message. A pen or pencil permanently affixed near the phone will help. Also provide message forms so that all important information will be included.

5. Remember that your voice gives the patron a mental image of both you and the library. Try to put a smile in your voice. Sound alert. Speak actively.

6. Use good grammar and diction. Do not use slang or "library-type" abbreviations.

7. Hold the telephone receiver correctly, about one half inch from your mouth. Do not carry on another conversation while talking with a patron. Never put the phone down without putting the call on hold.

8. Be of service; initiate offers of help. However, do not give information or refer callers to other areas unless you are absolutely sure you are correct. If there is any question about the best possible place to refer the call, take a name and number and tell the caller a staff member will call back with the proper information. Be certain to give the message to the staff member who can answer the question. Designate a staff member to handle telephone questions if it is not obvious to the student assistant where the message would go.

9. Never indicate that a staff member is on a break or at lunch if he or she is not in the office. Simply indicate that the staff member is "out of the office," and offer to take a message. Confirm the name and number. Promptly put the message in the staff member's designated message location. Vacations and absences should be clearly noted each day. If an absent staff member is requested by a caller, the student should ask if someone else can help.

10. Some staff members will want their calls "screened." You will be informed of those who prefer this service. This means that you should ask the callers' name, "May I ask who is calling?", put the caller on hold, call the staff member on the intercom, and give the callers' name. This allows the staff member the opportunity to mentally prepare for the call.

11. Always finish the conversation. Say good-bye and thank the caller, but always let the caller hang up first.

12. Do not leave messages on a desk or in a pile. Distribute them promptly. Write clearly on the standard message form. Include: to whom the message is directed; the date and time the call was received; the name of the caller (correctly spelled); the message; a return telephone number; and your initials. Provide message forms for the students to use. If there are any questions about the message the staff member will know who to ask. All staff members should have a designated location for messages to be placed.

Telephone etiquette is something that must be continually monitored, with frequent retraining. Short group sessions held throughout the semester will keep the telephone from becoming a difficult situation to handle.

Hostile Patron Situations

On occasion, students will be faced with "problem patron" situations. This may arise because of the students' inability to satisfy the patrons' needs, either because the rules prevent it, or because of lack of knowledge. Under these situations frustrated patrons often exhibit rude, obnoxious behavior. Students need to be trained to deal with problem patrons in an effective yet disarming way. This requires training the students in the fine art of dealing with difficult situations. A short training session could provide enough basic techniques for students to get through a difficult situation. Again, role playing is an excellent way to practice the techniques that can be described and given to the students in writing.

1. If a patron becomes irate and loud while you are dealing with him or her, attempt to determine the cause of the problem and to find a solution. While doing, this remain attentive and pleasant.
2. Lower your voice. Speak quietly. Very often the patron will become quieter if they are interacting with someone who is speaking quietly.
3. Listen attentively and take notes. Nod your head to indicate you understand. Empathize with the patron, but do not agree that library rules are stupid, etc. Keep your integrity.
4. Do not take the problem as a personal attack. However, if the patron becomes abusive while no supervisory staff are on duty, call security. (Supervisors: always provide to the students quick access to security personnel and let your security personnel know when you will have students alone.)
5. Use all information available to you and as much decision making power as is allowed you to attempt to solve the problem. Use the problem-solving techniques that you have practiced. Offer to turn the matter over to your supervisor. If the supervisor is on duty, find him or her immediately. If no supervisor is on duty, take down complete information including: the patron's name, address, and phone number; the nature of the problem; what kind of solutions you have offered; the date and time of the encounter; and your name. (Supervisors: provide forms for your student assistant to fill out giving the necessary information. This will provide the

student assistant a guideline to follow, the patron will know his or her complaint is being taken seriously, and a form will will cover the areas of information necessary for the report.)

Sometimes patrons can be calmed by simply listening to them. Other times, it is impossible to satisfy an irate patron. Do the best you can and then turn the situation over to a supervisor. In some cases, patrons can not be given the results they would like to see.

Emergencies

Emergencies are a part of every workplace, including libraries. Libraries can experience a variety of types of emergencies including fires, thefts, bomb threats, flooding, and medical emergencies. A well-trained staff, including student staff, can reduce danger to themselves, other employees, and patrons, and minimize property damage. It is therefore imperative that emergency procedures be spelled out, written down, and rehearsed so that they can be properly followed under severe stress (i.e., during a real situation).

A documented emergency procedure should be part of the operational plan of each organization. Basic procedures from this document, plus additions that speak directly to students, can form the basis for the emergency guidelines given to the student staff. The basic plan can be part of the procedure manual, given directly to each student, or both. However it is presented, it is necessary that the plan be reviewed by the supervisor with the students, and the emergency procedures practiced. This basic plan should include the following components.

Who's in Charge?

When students are working under a regular staff member, it is fairly obvious that the supervisor would be the one to report and handle an emergency. However, when students are working alone in the building, or are not working directly under a staff supervisor, clear lines of authority must be designated. To whom would they report a theft, a behavior problem, a medical emergency, or a fire? If or when students are working alone in the building or area, will one student be designated the student in charge, or will there be another way of determining who will seek assistance in case of an emergency? This must be clearly indicated to the student staff, preferably in writing before the first day of the student's employment.

What Is an Emergency?

Although it is impossible to plan for every emergency situation that might occur, it is helpful for the students to be given examples of what is considered an emergency, as well as how to respond to each. Types of emergencies may even be delineated by who should be called; i.e., the emergency number ("911" or "0") or the "regular" on-campus number for public safety. For example, for these emergencies, students might be instructed to call the emergency number: accident or illness; bomb threats; fires. For these emergencies, they might be instructed to dial the regular public safety number: behavior problems; locking building doors; power blackouts; thefts.

What to Do in an Emergency

Once an emergency has been identified, students need to be given an indication of what is necessary in the immediate situation. Some immediate responses, when rehearsed, can be employed by the student assistants to minimize property loss and danger to themselves and library patrons. One of the first things students must be instructed to do in certain emergencies, such as fire, is to communicate to the rest of the building what must be done. Emergency communications systems should be present and explained to the students for use in these situations. Second, students must be given specific information regarding each type of anticipated emergency. The following are some examples.

1. *Fire.* Use the fire alarm box and go to a designated area to await emergency personnel. If the fire is easily extinguishable, attempt to do so. (Students may be trained in the use of fire extinguishers.)
2. *Accident or illness.* Do not move the victim unless absolutely necessary. A first aid kit and blanket should be readily available and their use explained during training. (Instructing students to perform any but the most elementary first aid should be checked with the organization's attorney for liability.)
3. *Bomb threats.* Do not evacuate the building until instructed to do so by emergency personnel. Make a written record of the threatening call including time received. If necessary, follow building evacuation procedures.
4. *Behavior problems.* Persons creating disturbances should be asked to stop or leave the building. If they persist, call Public Safety. If they threaten an employee, call the emergency number. *Never engage in a shouting match with a hostile patron.*

5. *Theft.* Get as detailed a description of the incident as possible, including asking the victim to remain while Public Safety is called. *Do not try to apprehend or follow a suspected offender outside the building.*

Other emergencies, such as those created by bad weather, may require additional directions. Any emergencies that could reasonably be expected in a particular library or area should be explained. For example, if the library is in an area that experiences a large number of tornadoes, procedures for this emergency should be clearly explained.

Evacuation   Evacuation procedures should be in place for all employees and patrons of a building. These may include the use of an alarm, a public address system, or floor runners (pages). For student assistants who may be alone in the building, or with a limited number of supervisory staff, a clearly delineated evacuation procedure is imperative. It must include such important details as: who should be assigned to assist the handicapped out of the building; will someone (or several students) be assigned to check the floors to be certain the evacuation meeting location is covered; what is the plan for accounting for all employees? Included in the procedure should also be the reminder that during an emergency (especially fire or electrical problems) the elevators should not be used. This makes it especially important for the student assistants to know it is their responsibility to assist the handicapped, who may need to be transported from another floor to the main entrance or to an exit.

Notification   Following any emergency, appropriate reports should be filed by the student assistant so that the supervisor has a clear understanding of the situation. Report forms should be readily available. Students should know to whom the report should go, and within what time frame. If an emergency happens at 11:00 P.M., should the building supervisor be notified, or can the report be filed for the following day? Students should be expected to accurately report the emergency and to sign their names to the report so that any questions can be answered at a later time.

When training student assistants to handle emergency situations, consider doing some or all of the following:

1. Provide each student with a written copy of the procedures.
2. Keep a copy of the emergency phone numbers next to the phone. (Should the telephone not be operational during

an emergency, alternative communication options should be posted.)

3. Role play the emergency situations.
4. Practice the evacuation procedures. Ask your public safety expert to critique a fire drill.
5. Designate individual student positions that will be responsible for certain emergency operations. Make certain that those students filling the positions are clear about their responsibilities.

Be prepared for any emergency. Good preparation can save both the lives of students and patrons and guard library materials from serious harm.

In addition to these generic training items, each particular library location will have specific, content related items to be covered. Whether the students are trained in small groups, one-on-one with a supervisor, or with a peer, a variety of training techniques is essential. It is especially necessary that some "show and tell" be given along with written instructions so that students get information in more than one format.

Evaluation

The training program goals will clearly identify levels of skills that must be reached before students can be considered fully trained. Constant informal evaluation by the supervisor is necessary to determine exactly where each student is in the training program. Close monitoring of the work of each student (having each student initial what he or she does), checking the student's checklist regularly, and group meetings with structured question-and-answer periods can be useful devices for informal evaluations.

Trainers may elect to conduct formal evaluations of student assistants at regular intervals, similar to those used for probationary employees. Sometimes the formal evaluation will speak louder to the student (make a bigger impact) than the previous, informal ones. If formal evaluations are to be used, students should be told when they are hired that their performance will be formally evaluated according to a predetermined schedule. This may provide additional motivation for learning all aspects of the job. These scheduled evaluations can then be used to adjust training for individual students. If a large percentage of the training has been conducted in groups, this will provide an individual appraisal of each student's performance. Individual training adjustments can then be made. Trainers or supervisors may use tests that measure skills at a certain interval after initial training and time for practice. They may even use the same tests administered before hiring or placement. This technique can pinpoint a student's areas of deficiency. It can also tell where progress has been made and can serve as additional motivation for those students who have progressed nicely.

Evaluation conducted at regular intervals can reward students who have been diligent throughout their training. Those students who know their jobs and duties well can be given additional, more interesting assignments. Several good evaluations may help a student move from one level of work to another, such as to a student supervisor position. Good evaluations and new job levels often mean increase in salary as well. This certainly is motivation for the students!

Evaluations of student work performance that occur only when the student terminates employment do not allow the supervisor the opportunity to diagnose problems before it is too late—too late either for the student or the area of the library in which that student works. Trainers need information on performance early and regularly in order to best prepare the student to serve the organization well.

Evaluation of the Training Program

A formal evaluation of the entire training program provides necessary feedback for these planning and carrying out training. They need to know what works and what doesn't, as well as whether the material covered is both appropriate and sufficient. Was the training program well planned? Were appropriate methods and tools used? Did the trainers find that the training program could be effectively administered? Did evaluations of student performance provide appropriate feedback on the effectiveness of the training? And, finally, were all components of the training cycle carefully reviewed when evaluating the program as a whole? The training program will come full cycle once the formal evaluation of the program is completed.

In-Service Training

While an initial training program for either an individual student or a group of students may be completed, all supervisors know that training never really stops. Trainers hope that one of the ideals being instilled in the students is a constant need for "continued" or "lifelong" learning. There are always new twists to every job. A machine is added, and one is taken away. A change in procedure occurs because someone has developed a better way to do it. Librarians constantly need to remind those working with the public that libraries are a *service* organization. In every library area the need is there for in-service or continuing education.

Continuing or in-service education should be treated as seriously as initial training. It needs a clear definition of its purpose, as well as a defined schedule. Review of previously covered topics as well as new topics is always appropriate.

The schedule and actual type of training may vary vastly from area to area within the library organization. Some areas, such as technical services, may need in-service training infrequently—only if and when a new technique is to be used or procedures are being changed or updated. In the circulation area, however, where automated systems may call for frequent changes, training may well take place daily, every few weeks, or every few months.

Continuing education may take place individually or in groups. Supervisors (or trainers) may determine that training for one new procedure does not warrant a group session. It may be best handled one-on-one or through the folders or bulletin board. However, some way must be determined to be certain that all students who need to know the new procedure read the notice or are otherwise contacted. Trainers need a report form that indicates that each student has the information and understands it. Understanding might well be the most critical element.

Continuing education sessions are an excellent way to provide information while informally checking the information students currently have. In addition to the new material being presented, the students can also receive an update and review of information presented earlier. This provides additional opportunities for students to learn the information necessary for the unit procedures.

In-service or continuing education sessions should be evaluated in terms of the goals of the sessions. Did students fully understand what was being communicated? If not, why not? How can these sessions be changed to provide more meaningful interaction and discussion? Have the students complete a short evaluation form in order to appreciate their perspectives. Other supervisors or staff members might be invited to sit in on the session and to give feedback on its content and delivery.

The Training Cycle

A complete training cycle encompasses all aspects of the training program, including planning, preparation, and development of materials, administering the training, evaluating the students, and evaluating the training program (fig. 12). Once the entire cycle is completed it starts all over again, with a revised plan and new methods and materials. The program is ever-changing, always with the goal to better meet the needs of the students.

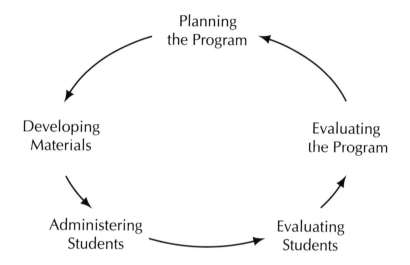

Fig. 12. This figure emphasizes the interdependency of the components of the training cycle and the need for consistent evaluation for the training program to be successful.

Chapter 5 Training in Special Service Areas

Depending upon the complexity of the library, special service areas will vary in number and size. While it is not possible to review all areas in specific terms, general areas will be addressed, including: technical services; public services (circulation); clerical; and special (microcomputer lab, language lab, audiovisual areas). A chart (fig. 13) is included that shows how training might differ from one area to another, and how it might also be the same. A brief discussion of all areas follows.

Identifying the Training Components

Commonalities

Preparation

The chart clearly illustrates the similarities and specializations of job positions within the library. No matter where a job is performed or what the job entails, basic preparatory steps must be completed before any hiring or training takes place.

If employees know how various jobs interact and understand their dependencies and the workflow, valuable time will not be wasted making sure "everything gets done by someone." This also eliminates repetitiveness, overlap, and constant frustration in trying to reach the end without the means being in place. By developing efficient and effective position-description statements, communication and expectation levels are easily and successfully maintained. Job functions, responsibilities, organizational relationships, and accountability are essential in all areas at all times, and will be if a basic foundation is laid in training preparation.

Job design directly affects the variable human side in basic job training. It is not an easy task to develop, in each position, duties that challenge but don't overwhelm, contribute to a sense of achievement, and allow for contributions to the decision-making process and transference of knowledge, skill, and abilities to one's life outside the library and into the future. The foundation in the design of job positions must be motivation. What can be put in each job that will make the person doing it feel that he or she is doing something important? What can each person do that he or she will be able to use outside of work? What in the job can be designed to keep the worker from becoming bored or careless? Remember that the basis for all motivation is "what can this job do for me?" Even when one assignment is used as a stepping stone to a better assignment, motivation is in place.

Along with a clear-cut knowledge of the job's description and its effective design, a job's objectives are fundamental and clearly acknowledged. Remember that the training objective is the most important component in any training process. Skills that are needed to fulfill each duty should be taught in a particular way to reach each goal. Priorities should now be obvious and goals attainable. Needs are defined, in place, and ready to be fulfilled.

In addition to defining jobs and writing job descriptions, other training preparations should be made before the hiring process begins. The determination of both appropriate and necessary rules and regulations and comprehensive training checklists is an important preparatory step.

While the concept of why these steps are necessary remains constant for all training areas, some of the specifics will vary from department to department. Usually all departments within a system will have some standard rules and regulations that apply to every student worker. There may be a requirement of the main hiring authority (if this is not the library itself), as well as regulations established by the library for all employees. Often the training and hiring are departmentalized, but standard procedures remain constant for all students hired by the main authority (i.e., the library). For example, it may be that every student hired by the library must present an authorization card from the institutional hiring authority (or a work permit and social security card). These are standard rules (or procedures) that must be followed by all students. The main department (or library) may also have standard procedures and policies that all workers must follow.

		Similarities	Tech Services	Public Services Circulation	Clerical	Special
Preparation						
	Job Description	Function Responsibilities Organizational relationships Accountability				
	Job Design	Duties: Challenge, not overwhelm Achievement Control or decisions Transferability				
	Objectives	Skills and duties What is taught, and how? Criteria to be met? Needs defined?				
	Rules and Regulations	Institution (Hiring Authority) Library				
	Training Checklists	Relate to Objectives Logical sequence Each job				
Hiring	Application	Skills Background Experience Interests Goals	Computer skills and kinds Math background Call number system Attention to detail Alphabet	Customer service experience Typing/word processing Verbal skills	Computer skills Typing/wp/math Public relations (some cases) Detail work Telephone Maturity Written skills	Machine skills—operating and repair Background in computers Understand nonprint sources

Interview	Explain job requirements / Information about organization / Information about student	Like detail work? / Lack of public contact?	Comfort with the public? / Verbal skills	Similar tasks?	Do you like to work with machines? / Variety of tasks?
Testing	Could be developed for each area / Type of skills measured would differ / What type of test?	Detail / Library knowledge / Math skills / Typing / Computer skills / Alphabet	Alphabet / Library knowledge / Relational/logical / Written/verbal / Simulation / Math skills	Language or English-speaking ability / Typing / Verbal	Used for placement—higher skill level / Machine aptitude—hands-on
Planning	Knowledge of job / Teaching/learning process / Order of training topics	Logical sequence	Priority needs		Sequence for understanding / Role playing
Training Tools and Methods	Manual / Handouts / Posting / Programmed Instruction (CAI) / A-V and flipcharts	CAI (programmed instruction) / Simulation or role playing / Drill and Practice	Video / Role Playing	Simulation— telephone etiquette / CAI (tutorials)	Simulation / Small group lectures
Evaluation Workers	Motivation / During/End / Met objectives? / Enhance goals? / Tests / Future promotions / Pay increases				
Program	How well do employees perform? / Judge effectiveness / What changes? / Training methods?				

Fig. 13. This chart emphasizes the generic relationship of student library positions and the need for specifics in many positions.

These may include: punching the time clock; turning in and signing time cards; and signing for paycheck pick up.

The variations in the rules and regulations need to be explicitly stated by each area. Technical services will be less restrictive than special service areas. All areas will include items regarding punctuality, dependability, and a statement about work expectations. However, in the technical services areas it may not be mandatory to find a substitute for hours not being worked. In a public service area, such as circulation, and in the special service areas such as a microcomputer lab, it will be imperative for students to arrange for their hours to be covered if they will not be working them. In some areas, such as offices, it may be a one or two student operation, and as such, no one would be available for substitution.

Likewise, with the training checklist there will be items that reflect the above policies (rules) and that are standard throughout all departments. Each individual department will want to develop individual checklists, but there will no doubt be several items near the beginning of the list that reflect the policy for picking up paychecks or for turning in time cards.

Dress rules may also vary from area to area. The overall rule may be "no short shorts" or "no jeans with multiple holes." Beyond that, students working in public services areas may be required to dress in a less casual manner than others outside the public view. Students transporting or lifting equipment, as in the audiovisual or media areas, may need to dress appropriately for safety as well as appearance.

In some areas the rule demanding confidentiality may be stressed more than in others. Students working in the administrative offices will find confidentiality high on the priority list, while those in technical areas will find little need to be reminded of it. Public services and special areas may need to be reminded about confidentiality of records, and thus would find this a relatively important item.

Special service areas, including the audiovisual and microcomputer areas, will have specialized rules and regulations as to what students are able to handle. For example, in the media area, it may be clearly spelled out that students working alone in the area are not allowed to distribute equipment. This is often helpful for students being badgered by patrons requesting equipment at the last minute. Students are able to defer to this rule if necessary.

The training checklists will also vary from area to area depending on the nature of the student jobs. As previously mentioned, all training checklists will include an item that covers the rules and regulations area. Following that, however, the lists will be very different depending upon the area to be itemized. Checklists follow closely what is to be learned in each job. Depending upon complexity, the student jobs may have one or more checklists per job. Students may learn several areas as circulation assistants. Therefore, they will need to be trained in several steps. Each area will require its own checklist. For example, a student may start out with the general charging and discharging function, move from there to reserve and, at a later time, on to the overdue system.

In some libraries, one student may be required to know many different areas. In other libraries, especially larger ones, a student may always stay within one area. In special service areas, there may be a variety of functions, all occurring from one central location. In this case, the job might be defined as "lab assistant," but the details broken down into several distinct parts, or on several separate checklists.

As students gain experience and knowledge, they may move into more responsible, higher-level positions. It is important that the higher-level positions have checklists that do not repeat earlier training functions, but build on previous training.

Review of both the rules and regulations statements and the training checklists must be completed often and thoroughly. As the training program is evaluated, both formally and informally, it is worthwhile to evaluate the effectiveness of both items. Since both need to be written and printed before new students are trained, early review and up-to-date information is critical.

Hiring   While the actual hiring of student assistants may vary from area to area in a library, some basic principles in the application, interviewing, and testing processes remain the same. The application form must be developed to ascertain students' skills, their backgrounds and work experience, their interests and goals. Interviews should always be designed to determine if the students can fulfill the requirements of the job as defined. By explaining the job requirements to the student during the interview, the applicant is better prepared to relate components of his or her past experiences that are most directly applicable. By asking open-ended questions, it is more likely that the student-applicant will talk freely and share goals as well as experiences. It is also likely that the student will share some ideas about customer service. This information can be used to determine if a potential placement is accurate. In the September, 1989, issue of *Super-*

visory Management, Linda J. Segall says, "You can learn a great deal about a candidate's self-motivation, interest in and ability to learn, and a general philosophy of life if you properly phrase questions about the individual's education and background. The interview will also allow you to determine language skills (especially when English is a second language)." [1]

Tests, if given by the hiring authority, must be developed and used in a nondiscriminatory manner. If a particular area in the library desires to use a test to measure students' knowledge and skills, all students applying to that area must be tested. A test cannot be used as a weeding device that helps eliminate "undesirable" applicants. Tests administered to all applicants should be basic in nature, and carefully designed so that what is really being tested will be of some use in the hiring or placement decision.

In each of four basic library units, applications, interviews, and tests may need to be tailored so that information can be obtained that is helpful in knowing whether the student is capable of handling jobs in specific areas. In some cases, it may be determined that the student is capable (has the skills) of doing the job, but does not desire a particular kind of job, or may not feel comfortable in a particular placement.

Technical Services

In addition to the standard, basic questions on an application, technical services will need to know some specific items, directly related to the skills necessary for technical services jobs. Additional items on the application may include specific questions relating to the applicant's previous math or computer skills and background, the perceived attention to detail, knowledge of the call number system, and any other information the student wishes to give.

The interview for technical services would also want to cover some of these areas verbally, so that students would have the opportunity to discuss their skills and experiences freely. The interview is also an excellent time to determine if the student is most comfortable in a work setting with little contact with the public. If not, a more public area such as circulation might be suggested as an alternative.

Tests given for technical services jobs might be in the form of typing or computer tests. This testing would be a quick way of determining what the skill level might be, and how best to place the student. Simple alphabetizing drills might also be given, so that students could demonstrate how well they understand the alphabet. If the shelflist (or card catalog) is still being maintained, asking the student to put a few cards in call number order would quickly give an indication of filing (and alphabet) skill before hiring and training.

Public Services

Library public services areas, such as circulation and shelving, will make good use of the standard application. However, for public services areas, specifics must also be highlighted or added. Any previous experience the student may have had in customer service must be highlighted. What exactly did he or she do? Did he or she operate a cash register? What computer or typing keyboard skills does the student possess? In addition to these items, it is imperative that the application also include the student's class schedule and other time commitments or restraints. Public services typically has long hours that must be covered on a somewhat equal basis, making the schedule an extremely important addition to the application. A willingness to work nights or weekends is also important, and may be used in the final decision to hire one student over another.

The interview for public services (circulation) must include open-ended questions that allow the interviewer to determine how comfortable the student is with public contact. The circulation area can be a highly stressful one, with extremely busy times, as well as times when patrons' tempers are short. This is not the area for students uncomfortable with public contact. The interview is also an appropriate time to assess verbal skills, both listening and speaking. If the student will be answering the phone, can he or she be understood? Can he or she understand what has been said?

During the interview, open-ended questions can also be used to determine the student's appreciation and understanding of customer service. A good interview will allow the applicant to discuss how he or she might address some customer service issues. Students who have previously worked in fast-food restaurants will be especially able to deal with the issues, both positively and negatively.

Tests developed specifically for public services areas may be similar to those used in other areas with only minor differences. For filing purposes, it is good to test alphabet skills as well as call number knowledge. Tests of math skills may be important in case fines need to be calculated or change made at the cash register.

In public services situations, solving problems can be especially critical. Questions can be developed that measure a student's ability to think logically and solve problems requiring relationships. These types of questions are subjective, however, and should be used only to give an indication of those students who seem to have problem-solving capabilities.

Clerical Positions

The standard, basic application is very useful for clerical positions. Past work experience in office situations can help identify students who have worked with typewriters or computers. Particular attention should be paid to indications that the applicant has held positions of increased responsibility or positions where he or she may have developed telephone skills. Has he or she worked with word processing or other software programs that the library might be using? Is handwriting legible? Clerical positions in a library setting allow a student to work both with the public and behind the scenes. An application should point to those students who have no direct public service experience but also give the impression that they should be able to deal successfully with the public.

In the interview, cover the situations and learning experiences students may have had in an office situation. The applicant should verbally explain previous duties and responsibilities and make suggestions for dealing with specific situations or emergencies that may occur in an office. The interviewer will want to find out the level of typing and word processing program skills through questions designed to uncover the applicant's knowledge and abilities.

Tests for clerical jobs would generally be typing or computer tests involving specific word processing programs, spreadsheets, or databases. Verbal and written skills are very important in most clerical positions and should be tested to determine levels of strengths and weaknesses. A good test would be to have the student write a telephone message from a printed conversation situation. Can the handwriting be read, the message understood? Is it complete? Have major points been missed or information left out? Are numbers transcribed correctly?

Special Service Areas

Special service areas generally include the need for in-depth knowledge or abilities in a specific field or function. Media service areas, computer labs, mending and bindery departments all require more previous knowledge and skills of an applicant. An application form that would be used in these types of special areas would need to give the student ample opportunity to express these unique skills and past experiences. Questions such as the following might appear on specific application forms: Have you ever repaired library type equipment, i.e. photocopy machines, computers, projectors, lamination or photographic equipment? Have you ever tutored? Have you ever assisted other persons with computer operations? Have you ever worked in a book repair shop or bindery area? These types of skills are much too important to overlook, especially if they are overlooked because no one asked about them.

Interviewing students for positions in a special area should involve questions that uncover the applicant's level of competency. For example: Did he or she work in a book binding area, or only watch the counter? What type of work was done with machines, or was the work just photocopying? Many special areas also require students to work much of the time on their own. An interview should allow the student to express his or her ability to accomplish assignments or handle workflow as needed, rather than with direct supervision.

Testing in special areas is easily accomplished. If a student is to work in a book mending area, ask the student to mend a book. If a student is to assist other students with computer problems, set up varied situations for the applicant to work through. If the student is to show movies, have the applicant prepare a movie projector for viewing. Special areas, calling for specific skills, allow for these special tests to be designed and used effectively. It should be noted, however, that there may not be a large number of students who already possess these skills. Therefore, more general tests such as alphabetization or math (for fines and change) may be all that is required.

Planning the Training Program

Training programs for all library areas require careful planning. Each area must clearly evaluate what is to be taught and what the ultimate goal of the training will be. Attention must be given to the teaching and learning process, with an awareness that not all students learn in the same manner or with the same speed.

When planning training, each specific library area will look to the individual jobs to determine how best to proceed. The basic principle holds true for all, however. That is, clearly define each job so that a training objective can be developed. Answer the question: "What should this student be able to do after training is completed?" The second question logically follows: "How can this best be accomplished?"

Each area will determine the best training tools and methods for their particular needs. In planning the training, however, remember to plan for learner variations, for frequent evaluation of what has been learned, and for an evaluation of the entire training process.

Training Tools and Methods

Training tools and methods may vary from area to area within the library because some methods will be better suited to specific types of jobs than will others. However, all areas will probably offer some type of general training and will use at least some of the following tools.

Written training manuals, handouts, and training checklists have a place in all areas. The manual can be placed in a strategic location and used as a reference after training is complete. A written procedure manual could be substituted for a training manual if the procedures are clearly spelled out and information is clear. Students may all be asked to read some or all of the manual at various times during the training period. Handouts (in written form) announcing new services or materials and postings of news items or the "solution to the latest glitch" are always useful and a valuable part of on-going employee communication and training. The trainer will want to keep an orientation checklist for each student trainee (figs. 14 and 15).

In each area, it may be worthwhile to try to gather together as many employees as possible for one general session. This will serve many purposes. In a lecture format or with slides or video, students can be given an introduction to the entire organization of the building (or several buildings). They can be oriented to the "big picture" of the service organization, introduced to staff members, and can get a general idea of what happens in each of the departments within the organization in addition to the one to which they have been assigned.

An organizational meeting also allows the trainer to give general information once, rather than having to repeat it numerous times in a one-on-one situation. Questions can be answered in the group, again with the same answer serving many students at one time. Students who have questions but are uncomfortable asking them will benefit from general question-and-answer sessions as well.

The general get-together helps student employees meet one another and gives impetus to the team building effort. Camaraderie is an important aspect of the work situation. Students very often develop deep friendships with other student workers. This can be a big benefit for those students new on campus who have not yet made new friends or find it difficult to make friends.

Circulation Desk

Orientation/Training Checklist

Date

_____ _____ Check In Procedures   _____

_____ Overview of Operations   _____

_____ Rules and Regulations   _____

_____ Student Manual   _____

_____ Telephone   _____

_____ Charging Out Materials   _____

_____ Charging In Materials   _____

Fig. 14. Sample orientation training checklist. A generic training checklist may be used if the trainer has prepared handouts and examples for each of the above areas. Leave sufficient space for notes, future reference, etc.

Media Services
Student Assistants

Checklist for Training

____ Ask new student assistant if he or she clocked in.

____ Stress that assistant must put badge on as soon as he or she arrives and take it off when leaving.

____ Take assistant around and introduce to each staff and faculty member. Cover organizational structure. Date:

____ Show student manual and where it is kept. Date:

____ Always check bulletin board for messages.

____ Tell assistant that the first priority is to the counter, then the telephone.

____ *Absolutely no one except authorized employees is to enter through the back door or come behind the counter. No one except media services employees are to use our phones. Public and campus telephones are located* _____ . Date:

____ Explain opening back door for mail, etc. Date:

____ Explain telephone and how to transfer calls. Stress importance of complete, accurate messages. Don't interrupt staff unless call is urgent. Date:

____ Explain check in/check out board behind student assistants desk. If faculty or staff member has not signed out, try to locate before taking a message. Date:

____ Explain sign-in/sign-out sheet on counter. Everyone entering the department must sign in and out. Date:

____ Explain procedure for taking in money and receipts in detail; instructions are in drawer at front counter. Student assistants never give change unless a purchase is made. Ask for money before work is completed. Change is available at the circulation desk and change machines are in Room 208. Date:

____ Library is not responsible for vending machines down the hall. If someone loses money, send to Room 315, McKenny Union.

____ Explain how to process an audiovisual request from start to finish. Date:

Fig. 15. Media Services student assistants training checklist. This checklist is used by EMU's media services area as a combination orientation-training checklist and main regulations reminder. The manual and other information sheets supplement this training. Main training areas require a date noting when the training was completed. This type of checklist should be always available to both the supervisor or trainer and the student assistant.

___ Train on the computer. Date:

___ Explain opening procedures for those opening. Date:

___ Explain closing procedures for those closing. Date:

___ Explain transparencies. Date:

___ Explain laminating. Assistants must always sign a release form as well as the audiovisual request.

___ Explain pick-up areas for laminating, etc. Must call patron when work has been completed and ask patron to pick up. Make a note and attach to the material each time patron is called. Date:

___ Explain preview rooms. Preview rooms should not be reserved; they are on a first come, first serve basis. If patron insists on reserving preview room, give name to a supervisor. If all preview rooms are filled, patrons can preview VHS in ISC, Room 102, but they must leave video case and their student ID or driver's license with us. For regular previews, set patrons up in preview room. Always have them sign in and out and leave case on your desk. When they are finished previewing, place VHS and case in basket to be rewound and reshelved. *Only one VHS or film at a time to preview.* Date:

___ Keep counter area and desk neat and clean. Don't leave obsolete notes, etc., lying around.

___ Counter area is not to be used to cutting and pasting. Direct patrons to tables in the lobby.

___ Keep a good supply of forms, transparencies, etc., at the counter and on the table at all times. Supply should be checked periodically.

___ We don't give supplies out to patrons. Inform patrons that paper, pencils, pens, etc., are sold in Room 208.

___ Copiers are available in Room 208 and on each floor.

___ Rental typewriters, fax machines, and computers are in Room 208.

___ Assistants must work at least four hours at a time before they are entitled to a fifteen-minute break. Anyone taking a break on work time will be reprimanded.

___ Please call and ask for the supervisor if you are sick. Don't leave a message unless no supervisors are available. Assistant must work his or her scheduled hours or get another media service student assistant to work unless he or she is sick.

___ The first time assistant does not call or show up, he or she will receive warning letter #1; the second no call, no show, assistant will receive a second warning letter; the third time, assistant will receive a terminating letter.

Fig. 15 continued.

The friendships developed at work provide motivation for the students. Coming to work gives *them* something—a place to socialize (within work guidelines) and an answer to the question, "what's in it for me?" At the general orientation session time should be allowed for this socialization to occur. Refreshments could be served if the budget can handle it.

Students should always be paid for attending the orientation session. Due to conflicting schedules, more than one general session should be scheduled, perhaps one in the morning and one in the afternoon or evening. All students should be required to attend unless released by a supervisor.

The socialization aspect of the general session also provides students with other students upon who they may call for substitutions. While lists of student names and phone numbers should be made readily available, calling for a substitute is easier (and thus more likely will be done) if the students know each other. In the long run this also helps the organization.

Audiovisual aids can be useful in the general training session. A video of the larger organization, introducing students to all staff members, can be very helpful. It could also provide a good opportunity to introduce students to the chief executive officer of the college or university, or to the chairperson of the library board. If these people were in the library, they would be recognized by the student assistants. Slides, or a slide/tape program, would also be useful and can be updated easily.

Technical Services

Student assistant training for technical services positions may involve more one-on-one training than other areas. Often only one student will be working in a given position at one time. It will therefore be necessary to develop training tools that alleviate the repetition required when training students individually.

Computer-Assisted Instruction (CAI) may be a valuable tool for technical services. Since many technical services jobs involve some kind of computer use, using the computer to train students is a logical step. Ann Turner, in "Computer-Assisted Instruction in Academic Libraries," says that CAI works best when, among other things, the job to be taught involves computers and when trainees come from a wide variety of backgrounds.[2] Using computer programs that give the students the ability to practice what they are to be doing on the job can be extremely useful. Drill and practice programs can either be developed in-house or purchased. Although more costly than some training methods, these should be useful with little modification for many years. Of course, in order to make use of this type of training, sufficient access to computers is essential.

Noncomputerized drill and practice training is also useful for technical services jobs. Students can be given a task that closely resembles the tasks that will be part of their jobs. They should be given instruction, either written or verbal, that explains the job and the manner in which it should be completed. The supervisor and the student might complete the task together the first time. The student should then be given the opportunity to complete the task alone. Students might be filing shelflist cards, making adjustments on an order record, checking in periodicals, or looking up books on OCLC. After the student's work is carefully checked by the supervisor several times, the student should be ready to proceed on his or her own with only future spot checking necessary. There is direct motivation in any training process that takes the student from doing a task with a supervisor to the ultimate of being able to do the same task independently.

In a technical service bindery or book repair area, individualized instruction is also generally used. Very specific instructions and guidelines should be made readily available for each type of material and each procedure that the student assistant is likely to encounter. Repair techniques for library materials could be taught by first allowing the student to observe the supervisor repair specific items, and then allowing the student to try the repair technique on his or her own. With the varying types of paper, glue, and other unusual guidelines in repair and mending, specific checklists for the student to follow with each item encountered would be especially useful.

Public Services

The public services functions often require that a significant number of students be trained quickly at the same time. Therefore, it is helpful if students can see a video or slide/tape presentation about the nature of the work to introduce them to the tasks at hand.

Handbooks and written handouts are essential in any area where there are many procedures and rules to follow. These can be either given to the students or placed in areas easy for the students to access. For example, a list of book check-out steps could be taped to the counter where book charges are actually processed. The student worker needs this extra "security blanket" in the first days of a new job and will need to refer to this list less often as time goes by.

A training room can enhance training for public services positions by providing both a place for simulation and role playing and where students can be given hands-on instruction. Students can be given an overview and hands-on instruction of a computerized system and practice with actual situations. Another type of simulation and role playing that can be beneficial is in "customer service." Students should be given the opportunity to practice before they are faced with a problem situation at the desk. An easy simulation to arrange is answering the telephone. Give the students an actual telephone and a list of calls to which they must respond. Students can either work in pairs or in a group with the supervisor present. Students working in pairs can also role play problem patron situations. Students should be instructed in basic rules of customer service through a lecture, video, or handouts, and then be given the opportunity to react to these situations before working at the desk. One student "plays" a problem patron, with the "problem" identified by the supervisor ahead of time. Each student in a team should be allowed to respond as he or she would be doing in a real situation. During the role playing, the supervisor should be "floating" among the teams, giving them further instruction and encouragement.

The cash register is another good simulation tool. Students need to practice using a cash register, selecting the appropriate keys for the appropriate transactions, and making change once they have received payment. If possible, it is good to have a cash register in the training room where simulations of cash transactions can take place. If it is not possible to have a cash register available just for training, students must be given the opportunity to watch transactions at the desk, to practice making transactions under the careful eye of a supervisor, and to have a handout of directions close by at all times when operating the register alone.

Clerical Positions

Clerical jobs filled by students can also make use of simulation and role playing. Telephone technique is a useful simulation activity. Students must observe how the telephone should be answered as well as be instructed in its use. A short lecture or video explaining the intercom system, the hold button, and other unique technicalities not on their home instruments is helpful. Students must also be given instructions in the proper greeting when answering the telephone, what procedure to follow regarding forwarding calls to individuals and in taking messages. Samples of these items should be part of a written training or procedures manual. In addition to this, however, students should practice proper techniques through simulation before actually answering the office telephones.

Other clerical tasks may include using a specific type of computer program, either to process timecards or to type letters and forms. Many computer software packages come with their own tutorial disks. These hands-on tutorials can be extremely beneficial for student employees. (Learning new software can benefit the student outside the office as well, since the software package may also be used for classes.)

Special Service Areas

Special service areas within the library may have unique training needs. Some specific audiovisual tools will be used for such technical areas as media and photocopy services. Both areas will use the equipment to be learned as training tools. In media or audiovisual areas, a training room could be set up for individualized instruction on each machine to be learned. In a lab situation, step-by-step instructions for each machine can guide the student through an individualized session. The student can repeat the procedures as many times as necessary until all steps are learned. A group of students could be trained at once if each student started at a different machine and moved around the room. Students could also work in pairs and help each other as they progress through the various machines.

Photocopy service centers also require attention to machines. It is more difficult, however, to set up a training room, since photocopy machines are very difficult to relocate. However, students can be instructed in the operations of the machines during a "down time" with the appropriate instruction manuals. Knowledge of the specialized instruction manuals for each machine is also necessary so students are prepared for any machine emergency.

For all special service areas that have public service desks, practice with the cash register and the telephone will be necessary. Special service areas will also use training tools and methods similar to other areas for the overall rules and regulations. Each special service area may, however, also develop specifics that relate only to certain detailed functions.

Evaluation

Evaluating Students during Training

Special library departments such as audiovisual areas, microcomputer labs, or language labs may require some specific evaluation measures. Students may be required to perform specific tasks, such as loading software in a computer or threading a film projector, at scheduled intervals. This may be done one-on-one or in small groups, and again is done to detect those students who may be having difficulty. Evaluation such as this protects the library from having students who cannot service the needs of the clientele effectively, and protects the student from embarrassing moments. Some students may be ready to work alone, or to go out of the immediate area to service a need, sooner than others. Evaluation of readiness is critical during the first weeks of employment in all special areas.

Special service area trainers may find that some students simply do not have the abilities and skills required for more technical jobs. If several attempts are made to train the student using various methods and tools, and still no progress is seen, it may be time to move the student to another area within the library, or to suggest that the student seek employment elsewhere. The early evaluation of the students' performance prevents a situation from developing that is frustrating to the student as well as the trainer. The ultimate goal of training student library assistants is to give the students something they can use as well as giving something to the organization. If a student becomes frustrated with his or her job, it may prove to be harmful to the student's self-esteem and could jeopardize his or her success in school.

Evaluation of the Training Program

Early and regular evaluation of student assistant work performance should also be used as an evaluation of the training program. In every area of the library, it will be necessary to look at the methods of training, the student performance based on those methods, and to evaluate the program itself, looking carefully at the training objectives.

While the training programs may vary from area to area, the same basic principle remains the same: help students understand what they are supposed to be doing and how they are to do it. If this is not being accomplished effectively, look back at the program and attempt to determine the cause of the failure. Is it the student(s) or the program?

If students are leaving the audiovisual center not knowing how to thread different types of film projectors or change a bulb in an overhead projector, what is the reason? Is there a gap somewhere in the training? Do they need more hands-on drill and practice doing these things, or are these jobs the library should not expect a student to handle? This requires that supervisors take a look at not only the training program, but the job definitions as well.

It may be helpful to ask the students in each area of the library to evaluate their training programs. After all, they are the ones who benefit most directly and who will be able to give the best feedback. Although this might ultimately turn out to be a painful process, it can be extremely enlightening. Something the trainers think is presented very clearly and without complication may cause the students extreme frustration. The students may also wish to suggest ways in which the training might be improved. They are closest to the need to be trained, and also to the age group being trained, and may have insights that prove to be invaluable.

Changes to the training program in each area may be necessary, but should be made after careful scrutiny of all data. Evaluation of the individual students, evaluation of work performed, and evaluation of the program by the students themselves should all be reviewed. If the review warrants a change, the training program must be reviewed to determine how any change might effect the entire program.

Evaluations of the students and the program are so closely related that it is difficult to divide the two. Both are critical to the final outcome—a well-trained student workforce.

In every situation, training will be developed to meet the needs of the individual organization. However, the basic tenets of a good training program prevail, and are organized with service to the clientele as the first priority.

Student assistant training has been explored in today's library. New developments are creating an exciting picture for training in the future. New technologies are becoming more cost effective and easier to use.

The challenge of excellent student library assistant training has been presented. Now it is up to you. Good Luck!

References

1. Linda J. Segall, "Four Steps in Hiring Success," *Supervisory Management* 34:15 (Sept. 1989).
2. Ann Turner. "Computer-Assisted Instruction in Academic Libraries," *Journal of Academic Librarianship*, 15:352 (Jan. 1990).

Bibliography

Ackerman, Phillip L., Robert J. Sternberg, and Robert Glaser, eds. *Learning and Individual Differences: Advances in Theory and Research*. New York: W. H. Freeman and Co., 1989.

Ball, Mary Alice, and Molly Mahoney. "Foreign Students, Libraries, and Culture." *College and Research Libraries* 48:160–66 (Mar., 1987).

Bard, Therese Bissen. "Why Train Student Assistants?" *School Library Journal* 30:26–29 (Jan., 1983).

Beach, Dale S. *Personnel: The Management of People at Work*. 5th ed. New York: Macmillan, 1985.

Bemis, Stephen E., Ann Holt Belenky, and Dee Ann Soder. *Job Analysis: An Effective Management Tool*. Washington, D.C.: Bureau of National Affairs, 1983.

Bloomberg, Marty, and G. Edward Evans. *Introduction to Technical Services for Library Technicians*. 4th ed. Littleton, Colo.: Libraries Unlimited, 1981.

Bolles, Robert C. *Learning Theory*. New York: Rinehart, Winston, 1975.

Boone, Morell D. "Motivation and the Library Learner." In *Bibliographic Instruction and the Learning Process*. Edited by Carolyn Kirkendall. Ann Arbor, Mich.: Pierian Press, 1984.

Boyett, Joseph H., and Henry P. Conn. *Maximum Performance Management: How to Manage and Compensate People to Meet World Competition*. Macomb, Ill.: Glenbridge Pub., 1988.

Brown, Darrel R. "Sharpening Your Job Interviewing Techniques." *Supervisory Management* 30:29 (Aug., 1985).

Center for Business and Entrepreneurial Management, Saint Mary's College of Minnesota. *The Fifty-Minute Management-Supervision Library.* Winona, Minn.: Center for Business and Entrepreneurial Management, 1988.

Cheffee, John. *Thinking Critically.* Boston: Houghton Mifflin, 1985.

Childress, Schelley H. "Training of Student Assistants in College Libraries: Some Insights and Ideas." *Arkansas Libraries* 44:25–26 (Mar., 1987).

Cottam, Keith M. "Student Employees in Academic Libraries." *College and Research Libraries* 31:246–48 (July, 1970).

Cross, K. Patricia. *Accent on Learning.* San Francisco: Jossey-Bass, 1976.

Davey, William G., ed. *Intercultural Theory and Practice.* Washington, D.C.: Society for Intercultural Education Training and Research, Georgetown University, dist. by Intercultural Network, 1979–81.

"Dead Men Don't Use Flipcharts." *Training* 21:35–40 (June 1980).

Drake, John. *The Effective Interviewer: A Guide for Managers.* New York: AMACOM, 1989.

Dunn, Rita, and Angela Bruno. "Dealing with Learning Styles." *Education Digest* 51:43 (Apr. 1986).

Entwistle, Moel. *Styles of Learning and Teaching: An Integrated Outline of Educational Psychology for Students, Teachers and Lecturers.* New York: Wiley, 1981.

Fear, Richard A. *The Evaluation Interview.* 3rd ed. New York: McGraw-Hill, 1984.

Ford, Robert N. *Why Jobs Die and What to Do about It: Job Redesign and Future Productivity.* New York: AMACOM, 1979.

Fournies, Ferdinand F. *Coaching for Improved Work Performance.* New York: Van Nostrand Reinhold Co., 1978.

Gagne, Rovert Mills. *The Conditions of Learning.* 3rd ed. New York: Holt, Rinehart and Winston, 1977.

Gaines, James Edwin, Jr. "The Student Assistant in Academic Libraries: A Study of Personnel Administration Practices and Institutional Constraints." Ph.D. dissertation, Florida State University, 1977.

Gerber, Beverly. "Training at L. L. Bean." *Training* 25:85–89 (Oct. 1988).

Guild, Pat Burke, and Stephen Garger. *Marching to Different Drummers.* Alexandria, Va.: Assn. for Supervision and Curriculum Development, 1985.

Houston, W. Robert, ed. *Mirrors of Excellence: Reflections for Teacher Education from Training Programs in Ten Corporations and Agencies.* Reston, Va.: Assn. of Teacher Educators, 1986.

James, Wayne B., and Michael W. Galbraith. "Perceptual Learning Styles: Implications and Techniques for the Practioner." *Lifelong Learning* 8:20–23 (Jan. 1985).

Kathman, Michael D., and Jane McGurn Kathman. *Managing Student Workers in Academic Libraries.* 2nd ed. Chicago: Assn. of College and Research Libraries, 1983.

————, comp. *Managing Student Workers in College Libraries.* Chicago: College Library Information Packet Committee, College Libraries Section, Assn. of College and Research Libraries, 1986.

Keller, John M. "Motivational Design of Instruction." In *Instructional-Design Theories and Models: An Overview of Their Current Status.* Edited by Charles M. Riegeluth. Hillsdale, N.J.: Lawrence Erlbaum Assoc., 1983.

Kendall, Frances E. *Diversity in the Classroom: A Multicultural Approach to the Education of Young Children.* New York: Teachers College Press, 1983.

LaBelle, Charles, and Susan Bookbinder. *Finding, Selecting, Developing, and Retaining Data Processing Professionals through Effective Human Resources Management.* New York: Van Nostrand Reinhold, 1983.

LeBoeuf, Michael. *The Greatest Management Principle in the World.* New York: Putnam, 1985.

Lieberman, Ernest D. *Unfit to Manage: How Mis-management Endangers America and What Working People Can Do about It.* New York: McGraw-Hill, 1988.

McCormick, Ernest James. *Job Analysis: Methods and Applications.* New York: AMACOM, 1979.

"Maybe They Can't Read the Manual." *Training* 11:36–37 (June 1974).

Meihofer, Susan S. *The Student and the Learning Environment.* Washington, D.C.: National Education Assn., 1974.

Mitchell, Gary. *The Trainer's Handbook: The AMA Guide to Effective Training.* New York: AMACOM, 1987.

Naisbitt, John. *Megatrends: Ten New Directions Transforming Our Lives.* New York: Warner Books, 1984.

————, and Patricia Aburdene. *Megatrends 2000: Ten New Directions for the 1990's.* New York: Morrow, 1990.

Noel, Lee, Randi S. Levitz, and Diana Saluri. *Increasing Student Retention.* San Francisco: Jossey-Bass, 1985.

Pauk, Walter. *How to Study in College.* 3rd ed. Boston: Houghton Mifflin, 1984.

Peters, Thomas J. *Thriving on Chaos: Handbook for a Management Revolution.* New York: Knopf, 1988.

——, and Nancy Austin. *A Passion for Excellence: The Leadership Difference.* New York: Random House, 1985.

——, and Robert H. Waterman. *In Search of Excellence: Lessons from America's Best-Run Companies.* New York: Harper and Row, 1982.

Rawlins, Susan M. "Technology and the Personal Touch: Computer-Assisted Instruction for Library Student Workers." *Journal of Academic Librarianship* 8:26–29 (1982).

Sager, Harvey. "Training Online Catalog Assistants: Creating a Friendly Interface." *C&RL News* 47:721–23 (Dec. 1986).

Segall, Linda J. "Four Steps in Hiring Success." *Supervisory Management* 34:12–18 (Sept. 1989).

Stone, Florence M., ed. *The AMA Handbook of Supervisory Management.* New York: American Management Assn., 1989.

Stueart, Robert D., and John Taylor Eastlick. *Library Management.* 2nd ed. Littleton, Colo.: Libraries Unlimited, 1981.

Turner, Ann. "Computer-Assisted Instruction in Academic Libraries." *Journal of Academic Librarianship* 15:352–54 (Jan. 1990).

Walsh, Rich, and Doug Soat. "How Trainees Learn." *Training* 12:40–41 (June 1975).

Wayman, Sally B. "The International Student in the Academic Library." *Journal of Academic Librarianship* 9:336–41 (1984).

Werther, William B., and Keith Davis. Human Resources and Personnel Management. New York: McGraw-Hill, 1989.

White, Emilie C. "Student Assistants in Academic Libraries: From Reluctance to Reliance." *Journal of Academic Librarianship* 11:93–97 (May 1987).

Williams, William H. "Factors Relating to the Employment of Student Assistants in Major American College and University Libraries." Master's thesis, Brigham Young University, 1969.

Willingham, William, John W. Young, and Margaret M. Morris. *Success in College: The Role of Personal Qualities and Academic Ability.* New York: College Board Pubs., 1985.

Wlodkowski, R. J. *Enhancing Adult Motivation to Learn: A Guide to Improving Instruction and Increasing Learner Achievement.* San Francisco: Jossey-Bass, 1985.

Zemke, Ron, and Susan Zemke. "30 Things We Know for Sure about Adult Learning." *Training* 27:57–61 (July 1988).

Index

Prepared by M. J. Anderson

Handouts, 48–49, 64, 90, 95
Hands-on learning, 19, 20
Hearing, 19
Hiring, 33, 41–43, 85–86
Hostile patron situations, 72–73
Hypermedia, 51, 52
Hypertext, 51, 52, 54
Hypothetical situations, in interviews, 42

I

IBM Windows, 51, 52
Icon-based systems, 51
Illness, 32, 74
Imagery, 23
Imitation, 7
Impulsive learners, 20, 21
In-service training, 77–78
Individual training, 21
Influence, personal, 13
Information-gathering techniques, in job analysis, 29
Instruction, individual, 2
Instructional design, 5, 11, 51
Intention to remember, 23
Interactive learning, 19
Interactive video, 50, 54–55
Interest, motivated, 12, 23
Interface devices, 54
Interrogative interview, 41
Interview checklist, sample, 44
Interview outline, sample, 45
Interview process, 33, 41–43
Interview questioning techniques, 21–22
Interview review, sample, 46
Interviews, 85–86, 87, 88, 89
  guidelines for, 42
  in job analysis, 29
  types of, 41–42

J

Job analysis, 29
Job dependencies, 28
Job descriptions, 5, 28–30, 64
Job design, 12–13, 30–31, 81
Job objectives, 81

Job progress, 42
Job routines, 50

K

Keller, John M., 11–16
Kinesthesia, 19, 20

L

Labelle, Charles, 30
Language barriers, 6, 7
LCD computer projection devices, 54
Leadership experience, 42
Leadership role, of trainer, 66
Learning, 21–24
Learning styles, 7, 16–24
Lectures, 20, 49
Leniency, 57
Lifelong learning, 77–78
Listening, 8, 19, 70
Literature review, 2–3
LOEX Clearinghouse, 51
Logical thinking skills, 4, 5, 21

M

MacIntosh hypermedia, 51
Manuals, 48, 67
Mathematical skills tests, 87
McHale, Cecil, 2
Media service areas, 88–89, 97
Memorization techniques, 22
Memory, 20–21
Mending/bindery departments, 88–89
Messages, 70, 71
Microcomputer areas, 84
Mistakes, learning from, 17–18
Mitchell, Gary, 16–17
Modalities, learning style, 18–21
Motion, and learning, 19, 20
Motivated interest, 23
Motivation, 5, 6, 10–16, 30, 81
Multimedia presentations, 55

N

Needs, and motivation, 12
Notification. *See* Reporting
NOTIS library system, 51

Morell D. Boone is professor and dean of Learning Resources and Technologies at Eastern Michigan University. He has a B.S. from Kutztown State University, and M.L.S. and Ph.D from Syracuse University. Boone has been a senior academic administrator for 18 years. He is also involved with research in and teaching new technologies for the transfer of information. He serves as adjunct lecturer in the School of Information and Library Studies at the University of Michigan.

Since very early in her career, Sandra G. Yee has been interested in the learning process, first as a reference librarian developing bibliographic instruction programs, and later as a library administrator. She has a Bachelor of Arts and Master of Library Science from Western Michigan University, and an Ed.D. degree in Educational Administration and Supervision from the University of Michigan. Yee is currently department head of the University Library at Eastern Michigan University.

Many years of supervising student library assistants provided Rita Bullard with the impetus to address the need for more clearly defined training. She has a Bachelor of Science and Master of Science from Eastern Michigan University and an A.M.L.S. from the University of Michigan. As a former circulation supervisor and currently a professional librarian at Eastern Michigan University, Bullard continues to provide leadership in the training and management of student assistants.